Dedication

To you, the reader, who has embarked on this journey of discovery with an open heart and mind. Within these pages, you'll find more than just words; you'll find a reflection of your own commitment to understanding, growth, and the pursuit of excellence. Your quest for knowledge and your unwavering curiosity stands as a testament to the boundless spirit of inquiry that propels humanity forward.

To my students, past, present, and future: Each of you holds a special place in the narrative of this work. Your questions, challenges, dreams, and aspirations have breathed life into this endeavor. You are the pulse behind every lesson crafted, every thought refined, and every concept explored. Your passion, curiosity, and resilience have consistently illuminated the path, serving as both a compass and a beacon. You've not only enriched this work with your diverse perspectives but have also been an inexhaustible source of inspiration and motivation.

This book is a tribute to your journey and to the indomitable spirit of learning that binds us all. As you delve deeper into its pages, may it light your way, offering insights and igniting the spark of empowered leadership within you.

Introduction

In the complex tapestry of human interactions, leadership stands out as one of the most studied, revered, and debated constructs. From the echoing hallways of academia to the bustling corridors of corporations, the discourse around leadership is relentless and ever evolving. Despite countless seminars, courses, and books dedicated to the topic, a profound question remains: What lies at the very core of leadership? This book, "Empowerment from Within," seeks to provide a perspective that is often overshadowed in the clamor for strategies and techniques – the psychology of leadership.

The realm of psychology is a vast and intricate field that dives deep into the nuances of human behavior, emotion, cognition, and motivation. It endeavors to unravel the tapestry of our minds, examining the threads of thought, feeling, and drive that collectively weave our individual and collective experiences. This multifaceted study not only provides insights into why we act the way we do but also offers glimpses into our vast potential, often untapped.

When one takes these rich insights from psychology and merges them with the practices and principles of leadership, the result is nothing short of transformative. This convergence brings forth a new dimension in leadership—one that goes beyond mere managerial tactics or strategic acumen. It heralds a leadership paradigm rooted in deep self-awareness, empathy, and a profound understanding of human dynamics.

In this intersection of psychology and leadership, leaders are equipped not only with tools to influence and guide but also with a mirror to introspect and evolve. By understanding the underlying motivations, fears, desires, and aspirations of oneself and those they lead, leaders can craft approaches that resonate on a profoundly human level. This isn't just about enhancing one's capability to lead; it's about redefining what leadership truly means.

When leaders harness the power of psychological insights, they move beyond surface-level interactions. They engage deeply, communicate authentically, and inspire genuinely. They are able to discern not just what individuals do, but why they do it, unlocking avenues for growth, collaboration, and innovation that might otherwise remain hidden. In essence, the melding of psychology and leadership doesn't just refine leadership—it elevates and transforms it into a deeply human-centric endeavor.

"Empowerment from Within" is an odyssey into the human mind, framed within the context of leadership. It's an invitation to explore not just the external world of leading teams, making decisions, and influencing outcomes but also the internal world of values, emotions, and cognitions. It's about recognizing that true leadership isn't about power, titles, or hierarchies, but about fostering growth, igniting passion, and nurturing potential - both within oneself and in others.

In this book, we traverse historical landscapes to understand how our perspective on leadership has evolved over time, reflecting societal shifts and emerging paradigms. From the dominant Great Man (Person) Theory, which romanticized inherent leadership qualities, to the more inclusive and holistic modern approaches that recognize leadership in its myriad forms, the journey is both enlightening and transformative.

At its heart, "Empowerment from Within" is more than an academic exercise or a compendium of leadership theories and concepts. While it does draw from a rich tapestry of scholarly work, its essence lies in its applicability. This book stands as a practical guide, meticulously tailored to resonate with the evolving dynamics of our contemporary world—a world marked by unparalleled diversity, rapid technological advancements, and an ever-shifting socio-cultural landscape.

Today's leaders navigate a terrain vastly different from those of previous generations. The rise of digital platforms, global networks, and instant communication has blurred traditional boundaries, ushering in opportunities and challenges in equal measure. It's a world where decisions are made at the speed of a tweet, where teams span continents, and where organizational cultures are as varied as the global tapestry from which they draw. Against this backdrop, understanding the psychological underpinnings of human behavior becomes not just an advantage, but a necessity.

Through the discerning lens of psychology, this book delves into the tangible challenges modern leaders grapple with. From understanding and steering the intricate web of group dynamics, where individual motivations and collective goals interplay, to the often-daunting task of making ethical decisions in an environment bursting with gray areas and moral dilemmas. It is not merely about 'what to do' but delving deeper into the 'why' behind actions and reactions, giving leaders a more profound understanding and thus, a more nuanced approach.

In an exploration of personality's role in leadership, we demystify how innate and developed traits shape one's leadership persona. Recognizing the bright spots, those qualities that inspire and drive positive outcomes, is as essential as acknowledging the darker shades of personality, which, when unchecked, can hinder progress or, worse, lead astray.

As our global community becomes increasingly interwoven, the traditional notions of leadership are constantly challenged and redefined. The diverse tapestry of humanity—with its myriad gender identities, cultural backgrounds, values, and experiences— necessitates a shift from a one-size-fits-all leadership approach to one that is inclusive and adaptive. "Empowerment from Within" champions this cause, advocating for a leadership style that not only acknowledges individual differences but celebrates and harnesses them. In this paradigm, diversity isn't seen as a challenge to be managed but a treasure trove of perspectives, experiences, and strengths that can propel teams and organizations to new heights.

We hope this book emerges as a clarion call, resonating with the urgent need for leadership that's not just knowledgeable but deeply empathetic and inclusive. At its core, it emphasizes the profound significance of truly grasping the intricacies of the human psyche. In a world marked by unparalleled diversity and interconnectivity, it becomes imperative for leaders to not just acknowledge but wholeheartedly embrace the rich tapestry of cultures, backgrounds, and perspectives that our global community presents.

More than a mere compilation of theories and concepts, "Empowerment from Within" stands as a manifesto for the leaders of tomorrow. For those visionaries who recognize that leadership transcends hierarchical roles or lofty titles, and instead view it as a sacred trust, a relentless pursuit of growth, and a commitment to making a difference. It speaks to those who are poised to redefine leadership, anchoring it in the principles of authenticity, introspection, and genuine connection.

By immersing oneself in the deep waters of psychological insight, leaders are better equipped to navigate the complexities of human behavior, motivation, and interaction. It is our fervent hope that as you journey through these pages, you'll be inspired to lead not just with strategic acumen, but with a heart that understands, an ear that listens, and a vision that seeks to uplift and empower.

So, as you turn the page, you're not just beginning a reading endeavor—you're embarking on a transformative expedition of self-discovery, enlightenment, and growth. Welcome to the heart of leadership, to the soul of empowerment, welcome to "Empowerment from Within."

The Psychology-Leadership Connection

The intricate dance between psychology and leadership is a fascinating one. Both disciplines dive deep into the study of human behavior, albeit from different angles. While leadership focuses on guiding and influencing individuals and groups towards a common goal, psychology seeks to understand the mechanisms of the human mind, emotions, and behaviors.

Leadership is as much an art as it is a science, and at its heart lies the enigma of human behavior. In a rapidly changing world with diverse challenges and opportunities, leaders who truly comprehend the myriad facets of human behavior are better equipped to lead with empathy, resilience, and agility. People are complex entities, driven by a cocktail of intrinsic and extrinsic motivations, past experiences, cultural backgrounds, and personal aspirations.

The psychology of leadership refers to the study of how psychological processes influence the abilities, behaviors, and characteristics of individuals in leadership roles. This field explores the underlying mechanisms that drive leadership effectiveness, including cognitive processes, emotional intelligence, motivation, interpersonal dynamics, and decision-making. By examining the mental and emotional constructs that underpin leadership behaviors, the psychology of leadership seeks to understand the traits and behaviors that make individuals effective leaders and how these can be developed and enhanced. It also delves into the impact of leadership styles on followers, teams, and organizations, aiming to optimize both leader performance and overall organizational success.

Understanding Human Behavior

For a leader, understanding this kaleidoscope of human drives is paramount. When leaders can anticipate how team members might react in a given situation, or what might motivate them to perform at their peak, they position themselves to bring out the best in each individual.

For instance, while one team member might be motivated by public recognition, another might be driven by personal growth and learning opportunities. Recognizing and addressing these nuances can help a leader create an environment where individuals feel understood, recognized, and motivated to achieve common goals.

Psychological principles offer insights into how individuals perceive the world around them, how they process information, and how they relate to others. Knowledge of concepts such as cognitive dissonance, self-efficacy, and attribution theory can be invaluable for leaders in managing team dynamics, navigating challenges, and fostering a positive work environment.

An understanding of human behavior also aids leaders in conflict resolution. Conflicts, often seen as hurdles, can actually be transformative if managed well. By understanding the root causes of conflicts, which often lie in unmet needs or misaligned perceptions, leaders can address the core issues, leading to stronger team cohesion and enhanced productivity.

In a nutshell, a deep dive into the realm of human behavior offers leaders a compass, guiding them in their interactions, decisions, and strategies. In a world where human capital is the most valuable asset, leaders who truly 'get' people stand out and drive unprecedented success.

At the core of leadership lies the intricate web of decision-making, a process often shaped by a combination of rational analyses, intuition, past experiences, and cognitive biases. In the dynamic and ever-evolving landscapes of businesses and organizations, leaders are frequently faced with situations that demand swift and impactful decisions. These decisions, while seemingly routine, often shape the trajectories of projects, influence organizational culture, and even determine the long-term viability of an entity.

Psychology

Psychology is the scientific study of the mind and behavior. It encompasses a broad range of topics, from basic processes such as cognition, emotion, and perception to more complex topics like personality, human development, mental disorders, and social interactions. Through systematic observation and experimentation, psychology aims to understand, predict, and often influence thought, feeling, and behavior across diverse contexts.

Leadership

Leadership refers to the ability or process of influencing and guiding individuals, teams, or entire organizations towards achieving a common goal or mission. It is not just about holding a position of authority, but involves inspiring, motivating, and setting a direction for others to follow. Leadership encompasses various styles and approaches, and effective leadership often requires a blend of personal attributes, skills, and situational adaptability.

Cognitive Processes in Decision Making

One of the most influential factors in decision-making is the way our brains process information. Cognitive psychology delves deep into these processes, uncovering the mechanisms that influence how we perceive, think, remember, and decide. By acquainting themselves with the tenets of cognitive psychology, leaders can sharpen their decision-making skills, ensuring that their choices are well-informed and effective.

Consider the concept of 'heuristics' – mental shortcuts our brains use to quickly process information. While they can speed up decision-making, heuristics can also introduce errors or biases. Leaders aware of such biases, like the *confirmation bias* (favoring information that confirms one's pre-existing beliefs) or the *anchoring effect* (relying too heavily on the first piece of information encountered), can take steps to counteract their influence, leading to more balanced and objective decisions.

Another pertinent concept is the framing effect, which dictates how the presentation of information can influence our choices. A savvy leader understands that the way a problem or solution is framed can drastically alter perceptions and decisions. By being conscious of framing, leaders can communicate more effectively, presenting information in ways that align with organizational goals and values.

Cognitive overload, a situation where an individual is inundated with too much information, can impede effective decision-making. By recognizing the signs of cognitive overload, leaders can streamline information, prioritize key data points, and ensure that decisions are made based on a clear and focused understanding of the situation at hand.

It's essential for leaders to cultivate an environment that encourages diverse viewpoints and constructive feedback. Such an environment can act as a safeguard against tunnel vision or groupthink, where the desire for conformity results in suboptimal decisions.

By integrating insights from cognitive psychology into their decision-making toolkit, leaders not only fortify their choices against common pitfalls but also pave the way for innovative, strategic, and forward-thinking decisions that propel their teams and organizations to new heights.

Highlights of the Psychology-Leadership Connection

Understanding Human Behavior
Effective leadership is hinged on the ability to understand, predict, and influence human behavior. Leaders often find themselves at the helm of diverse teams, each individual bringing with them a unique set of motivations, aspirations, and challenges. By tapping into psychological principles, leaders can tailor their approach to meet the unique needs of each team member, thereby ensuring that every individual feels valued and inspired to contribute their best.

Cognitive Processes in Decision Making
Decision-making is a pivotal aspect of leadership. Every day, leaders make choices that can have far-reaching consequences for their teams, organizations, or even entire communities. An understanding of cognitive psychology can provide leaders with invaluable insights into how they process information, the biases they might carry, and the potential pitfalls they should be wary of. This knowledge can be instrumental in ensuring that decisions are made rationally, with a holistic consideration of all factors.

Emotional Intelligence
In the realm of leadership, technical prowess or strategic acumen alone isn't enough. Leaders need to be emotionally attuned – both to themselves and to those they lead. Emotional intelligence enables leaders to foster genuine connections, navigate conflicts with grace, and build a culture of trust and respect. This not only enhances team cohesion but also drives better performance and job satisfaction.

The Dynamics of Group Behavior
Leading a team isn't just about managing individuals – it's also about understanding the complex dynamics that play out when people come together as a group. Social psychology offers insights into phenomena like group cohesion, groupthink, and collective decision-making. By being aware of these dynamics, leaders can harness the strengths of collective wisdom while being vigilant against potential group biases or pitfalls.

Interpersonal Relationships and Communication
At the heart of leadership lies communication. It's the vehicle through which visions are shared, strategies are outlined, and feedback is provided. Drawing from communication theories and principles, leaders can ensure that their messaging is clear, persuasive, and resonates with their audience.

Emotional Intelligence

In the mosaic of skills that define effective leadership, emotional intelligence (EI) stands out as one of the most pivotal and transformative. While traditionally, leadership was viewed through the lens of authoritative command, decisiveness, and domain knowledge, the modern leadership landscape acknowledges the profound impact of emotions on human behavior and organizational outcomes. It's here that emotional intelligence casts its indelible mark.

Emotional intelligence encapsulates the ability to recognize, comprehend, and manage our own emotions while simultaneously being attuned to and influencing the emotions of others. This multi-faceted competency goes beyond the mere acknowledgment of emotions; it represents the marriage of emotion and cognition in guiding thinking and behavior.

Leaders endowed with high emotional intelligence exhibit a profound understanding of their emotional states. Such self-awareness acts as the foundation for self-regulation. Rather than being slaves to their impulses, these leaders can modulate their reactions, displaying patience in adversity, calmness in crises, and resilience in the face of setbacks. This ability is invaluable in ensuring that emotional outbursts don't compromise decision-making or relationships.

Emotional intelligence enhances empathy, granting leaders the capacity to perceive and relate to the emotions of their team members. Such leaders don't just acknowledge the contributions of their teams but also understand their aspirations, fears, and concerns.

They can gauge the emotional climate of their organization, enabling them to address discontent, foster morale, and cultivate an environment where individuals feel genuinely seen and valued. The prowess of emotional intelligence also shines in conflict resolution. Conflicts, often laden with emotional undertones, can escalate if not handled with sensitivity. An emotionally intelligent leader approaches such situations with an open mind and heart, striving for understanding and seeking win-win outcomes rather than resorting to authoritative decrees.

Emotional intelligence fosters authentic communication. Leaders with high EI are adept at providing feedback in constructive ways, ensuring that critiques are received not as personal affronts but as avenues for growth. Similarly, they are receptive to feedback about themselves, viewing it as an opportunity to learn and evolve.

In an era where teamwork is paramount, emotional intelligence plays a key role in team dynamics. Leaders who cultivate and embody EI principles foster teams characterized by mutual respect, open communication, and collaborative synergy. This not only elevates the quality of work but also enhances job satisfaction and retention.

While technical skills and strategic thinking remain integral to leadership, emotional intelligence is the bridge that connects leaders with their teams, their vision with reality, and aspirations with outcomes. In the dance of leadership, emotional intelligence is the rhythm that brings harmony, depth, and resonance to every move.

The Dynamics of Group Behavior

The tapestry of leadership unfolds not just in one-on-one interactions but prominently in the arena of group dynamics. Leading a collective is a multifaceted challenge, where the behavior, attitudes, and interactions of individuals coalesce to form patterns that are often more complex than the sum of their parts. Delving into the nuances of group behavior, leaders can unlock the potential of their teams, steer them away from pitfalls, and ensure they work synergistically towards common objectives.

One fundamental aspect of group behavior is group cohesion. This refers to the bonds that tie members together, instilling a sense of camaraderie and shared purpose. When cohesion is strong, teams tend to have better communication, greater commitment to group objectives, and heightened morale. However, excessively strong cohesion can also lead to a desire for conformity, which may stifle creativity and dissent. Leaders must strike a balance, fostering cohesion while also encouraging independent thought and creativity.

A byproduct of excessive cohesion is the phenomenon known as groupthink. This occurs when the desire for harmony in a group leads to unchallenged and poor decision-making. In such scenarios, dissenting opinions are muted, and the group gravitates towards a consensus without thorough evaluation. Leaders need to be cognizant of the signs of groupthink – such as the absence of dissent, a sense of invulnerability, or an unquestioned belief in the group's morality – and actively work to encourage diverse viewpoints and open discussions.

Collective decision-making is another cornerstone of group behavior. When done right, it leverages the diverse expertise and perspectives of group members, leading to more informed and holistic decisions. However, it's also susceptible to challenges like polarization (where group discussions lead to more extreme viewpoints) or dominance by a few vocal members. Effective leaders facilitate inclusive discussions, ensuring that every voice is heard and that decisions are made in the best interest of the collective.

Another intriguing dynamic is the social loafing phenomenon. It suggests that individuals, when working in a group, might exert less effort than when they work alone, primarily because they believe their individual contribution might go unnoticed in the group's collective output. Leaders can combat this by setting clear individual responsibilities, regularly acknowledging contributions, and creating an environment where each member feels accountable to the group's success.

The role of leadership itself influences group dynamics profoundly. A leader's behavior, communication style, and decision-making approach can either catalyze positive group behavior or exacerbate negative dynamics. For instance, a participative leadership style might encourage collective involvement and ownership, while an autocratic approach might stifle input and breed resentment.

Understanding the intricacies of group behavior is pivotal for leaders aiming to harness the collective power of their teams. By appreciating the nuances of group interactions, fostering open communication, and actively mitigating potential pitfalls, leaders can guide their teams to success with harmony and efficacy.

Leadership, at its core, thrives on the connections made and nurtured between a leader and their followers. These connections, while fortified by shared goals and visions, are primarily built on the bedrock of effective communication. The ebb and flow of ideas, aspirations, concerns, and feedback form the lifeblood of any thriving organization. Mastery over the art and science of communication elevates a competent leader to an exceptional one.

Communication is Key to Leadership

Communication is more than just the conveyance of information. It's a two-way process that involves understanding the nuances of both verbal and non-verbal cues. For leaders, every word chosen, the tone of voice used, and even the gestures accompanying their words can either fortify their message or diminish its impact.

Effective leaders know that listening is as crucial, if not more so, than speaking. Active listening, where leaders genuinely focus on understanding the perspectives and concerns of their team members, lays the foundation for trust. It signals to team members that their insights are valued, fostering an environment where open dialogue flourishes.

Drawing from communication theories, leaders can adopt the principles of clarity and conciseness. A clear message, devoid of jargon and ambiguity, ensures that team members are aligned in their understanding. Conciseness, on the other hand, ensures that the core message is not lost in a deluge of information. These principles, combined with the art of storytelling, can make a vision or strategy more compelling and relatable.

Feedback, an integral part of leadership communication, needs to be approached with empathy and precision. Constructive feedback can catalyze growth, while poorly delivered criticism can demotivate and alienate team members. By employing strategies such as the "feedback sandwich" (where critique is couched between positive comments) or by being solution-oriented rather than problem-focused, leaders can guide team members towards improvement while maintaining their morale.

Another crucial aspect is the understanding of non-verbal communication. Factors such as body language, facial expressions, and even the distance maintained during interactions can convey volumes. Leaders attuned to these cues can better gauge the emotional climate of their teams and adapt their communication style accordingly.

Understanding and respecting cultural and individual communication differences is paramount in today's globalized world. With diverse teams becoming the norm, leaders need to be sensitive to cultural nuances, adapting their communication styles to bridge differences and foster understanding. The dance of leadership is choreographed on the stage of interpersonal relationships, and effective communication is the music that guides this dance. Leaders who invest in honing their communication skills pave the way for stronger connections, smoother operations, and a more engaged and inspired team.

The Evolution of Leadership Studies

The study of leadership, like most academic pursuits, has evolved in its scope, methods, and theories over time. Its origins can be traced back to ancient civilizations, where discussions on leadership were often rooted in philosophical discourse and religious tenets. For instance, ancient Chinese philosopher Confucius mused on the moral foundations of leadership, while classical texts like the 'Bhagavad Gita' from India touched upon the duties and responsibilities of a leader in the face of adversity.

As societies grew and organizations developed, the study of leadership started to shift from a largely philosophical realm to a more empirical one, seeking tangible characteristics and patterns among successful leaders.

The dawn of the 20th century witnessed a burgeoning interest in the scientific study of leadership, with the trait theory positioning itself at the forefront of this exploration. As industries expanded and organizational structures grew more complex, there arose a compelling need to understand the intrinsic qualities that distinguished leaders from followers. This quest for understanding centered on the belief that certain individuals possessed innate characteristics that predisposed them to leadership roles, fueling the age-old debate of nature versus nurture in the realm of leadership.

The Trait Era in Leadership Studies

The trait era, in its essence, was rooted in the quest to pinpoint specific, inherent characteristics that defined effective leaders. Researchers of the time embarked on exhaustive studies, analyzing both historical figures and contemporary leaders in a bid to distill the quintessential traits that seemed synonymous with leadership prowess.

The premise was straightforward: if one could identify a consistent set of traits among recognized leaders, it might be possible to predict or even cultivate leadership based on the presence of these traits. This approach was underlined by the conviction that certain individuals were simply predestined to lead due to their inherent qualities, a belief that harkened back to the ancient notion of the "born leader."

While many traits were proposed and studied, several stood out as being consistently associated with effective leadership. Intelligence emerged as a critical factor, suggesting that leaders often had the cognitive ability to grasp complex situations, devise strategies, and make informed decisions. Self-confidence was another pivotal trait, highlighting the leader's belief in their own capabilities and their ability to inspire trust and confidence in others. Determination, too, was seen as indispensable, underscoring a leader's drive, resilience, and unwavering commitment to their vision. Moreover, integrity became recognized as a cornerstone trait, emphasizing the moral and ethical compass that guides leaders in their interactions and decisions.

However, as influential as the trait era was, it was not without its critiques. Over time, scholars began to question the universality of these traits. Was it truly possible to delineate a definitive list of traits that applied to all leaders, irrespective of context? Were there no leaders who defied these commonly accepted traits yet were effective in their unique ways? These questions marked the beginning of a shift from a purely trait-centric view of leadership to more nuanced approaches that considered situational and behavioral aspects.

Despite its eventual evolution, the trait era laid crucial groundwork in the study of leadership. It prompted rigorous inquiry into the essence of leadership, inspiring subsequent generations of researchers to delve deeper into the multifaceted world of leadership dynamics, behaviors, and contexts.

The Behavioral Era of Leadership

The progression of leadership studies in the mid-20th century witnessed a shift from the fixed confines of inherent traits to the more dynamic realm of observable behaviors. As organizations grew in scale and complexity, there emerged a need to understand not just who leaders were, but how they acted. The behavioral era of leadership, rooted in the burgeoning field of organizational psychology, sought to address this very aspect.
This shift in perspective stemmed from an evolving understanding that leadership wasn't just about possessing specific traits; it was significantly influenced by the actions and behaviors a leader demonstrated. Furthermore, this perspective provided a more optimistic and actionable view of leadership. If leadership was,

indeed, a set of behaviors, then it could be learned, practiced, and perfected. Thus, the notion of leadership shifted from being an exclusive realm of the 'chosen few' endowed with specific traits, to a domain accessible to anyone willing to learn and adopt effective leadership behaviors.

Central to the behavioral era was the identification and categorization of leadership styles. Drawing upon extensive observational studies and experimental research, leadership behaviors were grouped into distinct styles, each characterized by its unique set of actions and interactions.

Autocratic Leadership

This style was characterized by a leader's centralization of power and decision-making. Autocratic leaders often made decisions unilaterally, with little to no input from their subordinates. They valued obedience, structure, and efficiency, often leading with a firm hand.

Democratic Leadership
Democratic leaders, in contrast, emphasized participation and collaboration. They often involved team members in decision-making processes, valuing diverse opinions and fostering an environment of mutual respect and trust. This style was predicated on the belief that collective input led to better decisions and greater team commitment.

Laissez-faire Leadership

Derived from the French term meaning "let do" or "let it be," this style of leadership was characterized by a hands-off approach. Laissez-faire leaders provided their teams with autonomy, intervening minimally. While this could foster innovation and creativity in self-motivated teams, it could also lead to a lack of direction in others.

The emergence of these styles provided organizations with frameworks to understand, evaluate, and develop leadership within their ranks. Instead of searching for individuals with specific traits, organizations could now train potential leaders to adopt effective behaviors.

However, like the trait era, the behavioral approach was not without its challenges. Solely focusing on behavior without considering situational context or underlying traits could provide an incomplete picture. Undeniably, the behavioral era enriched the tapestry of leadership studies, introducing the concept that leadership was, in many ways, a skill to be honed rather than just an inherent quality to be possessed.

The Situational Era of Leadership

With the evolution of leadership studies, there came a growing acknowledgment of the intricate interplay between a leader's characteristics, their actions, and the environment in which they operated. As the limitations of both trait and behavioral approaches became evident, the spotlight shifted towards understanding the situational context of leadership. This transition marked the birth of the contingency and situational theories, which posited that leadership effectiveness was not just a product of who the leader was or what they did, but also of the circumstances they found themselves in.

Contingency Theory: Pioneered by researchers like Fiedler, the contingency theory asserted that the success of a leader wasn't universal but contingent upon the match between their style and the demands of the situation. In Fiedler's model, for instance, the effectiveness of a leader was determined by their leadership style and the favorability of the situation. Leaders were classified as either task-oriented or relationship-oriented and depending on situational factors like leader-member relations, task structure, and positional power, one style might be more effective than the other.

The core tenet was that there wasn't one "best" way to lead; instead, the effectiveness of a leadership style depended on the context.

Situational Theory: Building on the foundations laid by contingency theory, situational leadership took a more dynamic approach. It proposed that leaders could and should adapt their style based on the demands of the situation and the readiness or maturity of their followers. The situational theory recognized that different challenges required different leadership responses, and leaders who were adept at reading and adapting to these nuances would be more effective. For instance, a novice team member might need clear directions and close supervision, while a more experienced member might thrive with autonomy and a participative leadership approach.

The emergence of the contingency and situational era was instrumental in broadening the understanding of leadership. It shifted the narrative from searching for a singular, universal definition of effective leadership to recognizing the multifaceted nature of leadership success. By accounting for the external environment and the situational dynamics, these theories brought nuance and depth to the study of leadership, underscoring the importance of adaptability and flexibility in leadership roles.

This era also prompted leaders and organizations to be more introspective and analytical. Instead of merely adopting prescribed leadership behaviors or relying solely on inherent traits, leaders were now encouraged to assess their environments, understand the unique challenges they faced, and tailor their approach accordingly. In essence, the contingency and situational era heralded the idea that effective leadership was both an art and a science, requiring a harmonious blend of personal attributes, behaviors, and a keen understanding of the situational context.

The Relational Era of Leadership Studies

The relational era marked a pivotal shift in the study and understanding of leadership, emphasizing the interconnectedness between leaders and their followers. Instead of viewing leadership as a unilateral process, where leaders dictate and followers merely execute, the relational perspective underscored the reciprocal and co-created nature of leadership.

This era posited that leadership is not merely situated within an individual leader but emerges through the dynamic interactions between leaders and their team members. Leadership, from this vantage point, became less about position or title and more about the quality of relationships, mutual influence, and the co-construction of meaning and direction.

Several foundational principles characterize the relational era:

☐ Mutual Influence: Leadership is seen as a two-way street. Leaders influence followers, but followers also influence leaders. The dynamics of this mutual influence shape the direction, priorities, and outcomes of a team or organization.

☐ Shared Purpose: Leaders and followers unite around a common mission or vision. It's not just about executing the leader's vision but collaboratively defining and refining that vision based on collective input.

☐ Interdependence: The success of the leader is inextricably tied to the success of the followers and vice versa. Each party brings unique strengths, perspectives, and value to the table, and recognizing this interdependence fosters mutual respect and collaboration.

☐ Quality of Relationships: The strength and health of relationships become a primary indicator of leadership effectiveness. Trust, open communication, empathy, and active listening become central tenets of this leadership approach.

☐ Co-construction of Leadership: Leadership is not just a static trait or behavior but an ongoing process. It is co-constructed in real-time through interactions, negotiations, and shared experiences between leaders and followers.

In the relational era, leadership became more fluid, organic, and adaptive. It acknowledged the rich tapestry of human interactions that form the backbone of any organization or team. By placing relationships at the heart of leadership, this perspective highlighted the profound impact of collaborative efforts and the profound outcomes they can achieve.

The trajectory of leadership studies, from its nascent stages rooted in philosophy to its current evidence-based approach, underscores the complexity of leadership as a construct. As we venture further into the realm of classical leadership theories, we'll delve deeper into the nuances of these evolutions, drawing connections between past learnings and present applications.

Exercise: "Mapping Your Leadership Journey"

Objective: To foster introspection and allow you to recognize and articulate your own experiences with leadership. This exercise aims to help you understand the underlying psychological factors that may have influenced these encounters.

Reflection Time: Spend a few moments reflecting on your personal leadership experiences. Recall moments when you assumed a leadership role or when you found yourself influenced by someone else's leadership. Identify pivotal, challenging, or enlightening experiences.

Your Leadership Timeline: On a sheet of paper, sketch a horizontal line representing your "Leadership Journey Timeline." Pick at least three significant moments or events from your past that stand out in relation to leadership. Above each point, give a brief description of the event. Below each point, capture the emotions or feelings you associate with that particular memory.

Connecting to Psychology: Beside each event, try to pinpoint any psychological factors that might have played a part. Was the event influenced by aspects like motivation, group dynamics, or communication hurdles? Were there any cognitive biases at play? Think about the internal and external factors that might have been at work.

Gleaned Wisdom: Reflect on each event and jot down a key lesson or insight you extracted regarding leadership. Ponder over how that episode molded your perception or leadership style.

Group Interaction: Team up with a few classmates and share one event from your timeline. Discuss the psychological elements you've pinpointed and the lessons each of you drew from them. As a team, recognize common themes or patterns that emerge from your shared stories. Which psychological elements pop up most frequently? Are there lessons that seem to resonate with many?

Class Consolidation: As a class, we will regroup. Each team can present their identified themes or patterns. Together, we'll explore how these personal stories intersect with the broader spectrum of leadership psychology. How can personal narratives shed light on the academic concepts we'll delve into?

Continued Exploration: I encourage you to hold onto your "Leadership Journey Timeline." As we journey through this course together, revisit your timeline. As you become familiar with new concepts and theories, you might find additional insights that you can integrate, enriching your understanding of your unique leadership journey in the context of our academic exploration.

Chapter 1: Classical Theories of Leadership

Leadership, as a concept, has captivated the minds of scholars, professionals, and laymen alike for centuries. The urge to understand what makes one person stand out as a leader, while another remains a follower, is a puzzle that many have tried to piece together. Historically, from the tales of epic heroes in ancient civilizations to the modern-day CEOs steering global conglomerates, leadership has been an integral part of human civilization. The curiosity to decode leadership has led to numerous theories over time, each contributing a unique perspective.

In this chapter, we embark on a journey to explore the foundational theories of leadership that have shaped our understanding of the concept. These classical theories, spanning from the idea of predestined leadership to the intricate balance between traits, behaviors, and situational contexts, offer a rich tapestry of insights. They serve as the bedrock upon which contemporary leadership paradigms are built. By delving into these theories, students will gain a comprehensive understanding of the multifaceted nature of leadership and the myriad factors that contribute to its efficacy.

The classical framework underscores the journey from understanding leadership as a divine endowment to recognizing it as a blend of innate attributes, learned skills, and situational acumen. It is a testament to humanity's persistent quest to decode the leadership enigma, offering foundational pillars upon which contemporary leadership theories stand and flourish. As we traverse the annals of leadership research, students will recognize that our perception of leadership has not been static; it has evolved, adapting and growing richer with each passing decade. And while the leadership landscape continues to change, understanding its origins is crucial for those aiming to be the leaders of tomorrow.

The Great Man (Person) Theory

The Great Man Theory emerged from the tales and histories of heroes, warriors, monarchs, and influential personalities that seemed larger than life. Drawing from these narratives, early scholars believed that these exceptional individuals were preordained for leadership because of the unique qualities they possessed. The underlying assumption was that these qualities were intrinsic, rare, and evident from early life, steering these individuals towards destinies filled with grand accomplishments.

Historical figures such as Queen Elizabeth I, Julius Caesar, and Martin Luther King Jr., with their indelible marks on history, were often hailed as exemplars of this theory. Their seemingly innate ability to lead, inspire, and bring about change was perceived as evidence of their predetermined leadership destiny.

Yet, as compelling as these stories were, there were evident limitations to this perspective. The theory leaned heavily on heroic narratives, often sidelining the contribution of countless unsung heroes or the context that played a pivotal role in these leaders' journeys. Moreover, the gendered terminology reflected the societal biases of the time, rendering women and other groups invisible in the leadership discourse.

Over time, with societal evolution and the deepening of leadership studies, it became increasingly clear that leadership was not just a matter of destiny. The Great Man Theory began to wane, making way for more nuanced perspectives that acknowledged the role of nurture alongside nature in the making of a leader. Still, its legacy remains as it set the stage for the quest to understand the mystique of leadership, prompting deeper inquiries and more holistic theories.

Trait Theories

The shift from the deterministic viewpoint of the Great Man Theory to the Trait Theories marked a significant evolution in leadership studies. Rather than viewing leadership as a birthright, trait theories proposed that certain distinguishable characteristics or qualities could serve as predictors of effective leadership. This perspective emerged from the burgeoning field of psychology, which sought to understand human behavior through empirical and scientific methods.

Throughout the early and mid-20th century, extensive research was undertaken to catalogue these leadership traits. Psychologists and researchers employed various tools and methodologies, ranging from observational studies to psychometric assessments, to identify recurring traits among successful leaders. Common attributes that often-emerged included adaptability, assertiveness, emotional stability, and problem-solving abilities.

While some traits appeared frequently across various studies, there was a growing recognition of the diversity and complexity of leadership. Two leaders might both be effective but exhibit different sets of traits. This variability highlighted the influence of contextual factors—such as organizational culture, team dynamics, or societal norms—on leadership effectiveness.

Another critique that arose was the potential bias in trait identification. Traits deemed "essential" in one culture or context might not be valued or even recognized in another. Moreover, the focus on traits sometimes inadvertently overlooked the importance of skills, knowledge, and experiences that leaders acquired over time.

Despite these critiques, the trait approach was instrumental in moving leadership studies towards a more empirical and systematic direction. It steered the conversation from the notion of predetermined leadership to the idea that leadership potential could be identified, and possibly cultivated, based on discernible qualities. This perspective laid the groundwork for subsequent theories that explored the multifaceted nature of leadership, blending inherent traits with acquired skills and contextual nuances.

The Great Man (Person) Theory

In the early annals of leadership research, the Great Man Theory was among the foremost frameworks proposed. Rooted in the 19th-century belief system, this theory posited that leaders were born, not made. The name itself suggests a certain historical bias, implying that only "great men" were fit for leadership. However, as society progressed, it became evident that leadership wasn't exclusive to a gender or a certain kind of individual. This theory was based on the idea that certain individuals possess innate qualities or charisma that destine them for leadership roles. Figures like Napoleon, Abraham Lincoln, and Mahatma Gandhi were often cited as examples of "great men." While the theory was a starting point, it was soon overshadowed by more comprehensive approaches as research evolved.

Trait Theories

Building on the foundation of the Great Man Theory but deviating from the idea of predestined leadership, trait theories emerged in the early 20th century with the intent of identifying specific characteristics or traits that could predict leadership effectiveness. Researchers embarked on a quest to pinpoint particular traits, like intelligence, determination, and self-confidence, that successful leaders shared. The underlying assumption was that individuals with the right combination of traits would naturally excel in leadership roles. Over time, various lists of "desired" traits were developed, though there was never a universal agreement on a definitive list. This paved the way for a deeper exploration of leadership, moving beyond just inherent traits.

Behavioral Theories

By the mid-20th century, the focus began to shift from the traits leaders possess to the behaviors they exhibit. Behavioral theories advocated that effective leadership was a product of learned behaviors, not just inherent traits. Scholars began categorizing leadership styles such as autocratic (commanding), democratic (participative), and laissez-faire (hands-off). The primary goal was to determine which styles were most effective in various contexts. It was during this era that leadership started being seen as a skill that could be taught and developed, leading to the establishment of many leadership development programs.

Contingency Theories

As leadership studies matured, it became increasingly clear that neither traits nor behaviors could fully encapsulate what makes an effective leader. This realization birthed contingency or situational theories, emphasizing that leadership effectiveness is contingent upon the interplay between a leader's traits, behaviors, and the context in which they operate. The environment, team dynamics, organizational culture, and even external factors could influence the success of a leadership approach. Thus, there wasn't a "one-size-fits-all" leadership style. Leaders had to adapt based on the unique challenges and dynamics of each situation.

Behavioral Theories

As the landscape of organizational dynamics and team structures evolved during the 20th century, so too did the paradigms of leadership. The emerging Behavioral Theories shifted the spotlight from what leaders are (their traits) to what leaders do (their behaviors). This represented a pivotal change in understanding leadership, underscoring the belief that leadership prowess was more than just innate qualities; it was also a manifestation of observable actions and behaviors.

The advent of Behavioral Theories was marked by extensive research to classify and understand distinct leadership behaviors. Researchers delved into organizational settings, studying leaders in action, and conducting interviews, observations, and surveys. Through these studies, it became clear that leaders tended to exhibit patterns in their approach to leading, giving rise to the identification of various leadership styles.

The autocratic style, for example, was characterized by leaders who took charge, made decisions unilaterally, and expected subordinates to comply without much input. Contrarily, the democratic style was marked by collaboration, where leaders sought feedback and involved team members in decision-making processes. Then there was the laissez-faire style, where leaders adopted a more passive approach, allowing team members considerable autonomy in their roles.

These classifications allowed for a more nuanced understanding of leadership. It became evident that no single style was universally effective. Instead, the effectiveness of a leadership style was contingent upon factors like team size, nature of the task, organizational culture, and the maturity level of the team members. For instance, an autocratic style might be effective in crisis situations requiring swift decision-making, while a democratic style might thrive in creative settings where diverse inputs fuel innovation.

An important offshoot of the Behavioral Theories was the emphasis on leadership as a trainable skill. The idea that leadership behaviors could be observed, learned, and practiced opened the doors to the conceptualization and proliferation of leadership training programs. These programs aimed at equipping individuals with the right set of behaviors to enhance their leadership efficacy. It marked a democratization of leadership, suggesting that with the right training and mindset, anyone could cultivate effective leadership behaviors, regardless of their inherent traits.

Contingency Theories

The advent of Contingency Theories marked a pivotal moment in the realm of leadership studies. As the name suggests, these theories posited that successful leadership was contingent, or dependent, upon the alignment of a leader's style with the specific demands of the situation. The essence of these theories was adaptability; effective leaders were those who could seamlessly adjust their approach based on varying circumstances.

Central to the Contingency Theories was the acknowledgment of the complexity inherent in organizational dynamics. Every organization, team, or project came with its unique set of challenges, goals, and personnel dynamics. Moreover, external factors like market conditions, competition, societal norms, or geopolitical shifts could add layers of complexity to the leadership matrix.

One fundamental premise of Contingency Theories was that no single leadership style was superior in isolation. An approach that worked exceptionally well in one context might falter in another. For instance, a highly directive leadership might be beneficial in high-stress, fast-paced environments where swift decision-making is paramount. However, the same approach might stifle creativity in a research and development team where innovation and out-of-the-box thinking are critical.

Contingency Theories highlighted the importance of leaders possessing a keen sense of awareness. Leaders needed to be astute observers, gauging the team's morale, understanding organizational nuances, assessing external pressures, and then integrating these insights to tailor their leadership approach.

Various models and frameworks were developed under the umbrella of Contingency Theories to guide leaders in assessing situations and adapting their styles. These models often involved evaluating factors like the nature of the task, the relationship between the leader and the team, the degree of structure in the task, and the leader's position power. By analyzing these factors, leaders could strategically align their approach to maximize effectiveness.

Contingency Theories elevated the discourse on leadership from static models to dynamic frameworks. Leadership was no longer about having the right traits or mastering a set of behaviors. It was about fluidity, adaptability, and the ability to navigate the ever-changing tides of organizational landscapes.

The classical period of leadership serves as a testament to the ever-evolving understanding of what it means to lead. This period, spanning from the reverence of extraordinary individuals in the Great Man Theory to the multifaceted interplay of traits, behaviors, and context in the Contingency Theories, reveals a profound shift in perception.

Initially, leadership was often viewed through a lens of mystique and destiny, with certain remarkable individuals seemingly preordained to lead. However, as society progressed and research methodologies evolved, the narrative transformed. Leadership began to be seen less as a divine mandate and more as a confluence of distinct attributes and learned behaviors, adaptable to specific situations.

The classical era, in many ways, laid the groundwork for our modern understanding of leadership. It challenged pre-existing notions, democratized the concept of leadership, and emphasized the importance of adaptability and context. As we reflect upon this foundational era, it becomes evident that leadership is neither static nor simplistic. It is a dynamic blend of the personal and the situational, of the inherent and the learned.

In this foundational period, we see the beginnings of many themes that would later dominate leadership discourse, including the importance of self-awareness, the value of adaptability, and the recognition that effective leadership is about both the individual leader and the context in which they operate. The classical period, therefore, is not just a historical point of reference; it's a critical foundation, informing and enriching our contemporary discussions on leadership.

Exercise 1: Leadership Trait Theories: "My Leadership Portrait"

Objective: To delve deep into Leadership Trait Theories, enabling you to understand and reflect on the specific traits you possess and how they relate to leadership effectiveness.

Activity: Leadership Trait Collage

Materials Needed:
- ☐ A list of leadership traits derived from Trait Theories included at the end of the exercise (e.g., intelligence, determination, self-confidence, charisma, adaptability, etc.)
- ☐ Magazines, newspapers, scissors, glue sticks, and large sheets of paper
- ☐ Markers or colored pencils

Instructions: Understanding Leadership Trait Theories: Let's start by discussing the progression from the Great Man Theory to the Trait Theories. Trait Theories aimed to identify specific characteristics that effective leaders possessed. While many traits have been identified, remember there isn't a definitive list. That means leadership is multifaceted and varied!

Creating Your Leadership Trait Collage:
- ☐ On the table, you'll find a list of leadership traits derived from various Trait Theories. Reflect on this list. Which traits resonate with you? Which ones do you see in yourself?
- ☐ Browse through the magazines and newspapers. Cut out images, words, or symbols that you feel represent the leadership traits you identify with. This will allow you to create a visual representation of your leadership style.
- ☐ On your large sheet of paper, create a collage using the images, words, or symbols you've chosen. You can also draw or write

other traits or qualities you believe you possess that may not be on the list.

Group Reflection and Sharing:
☐ Once you've finished your collage, team up with 3-4 classmates. Take turns sharing your collages, explaining why you chose certain traits and how you perceive them in your leadership style or potential.
☐ Discuss the similarities and differences among your group's collages. What does this diversity tell you about leadership?

Debrief: The diversity in your collages underscores a key takeaway from Trait Theories: leadership isn't confined to a strict set of characteristics. While some traits may naturally lend themselves to leadership roles, the beauty lies in the unique combination each individual brings to the table. Always remember, leadership isn't just about the traits you're born with but how you nurture, cultivate, and leverage them throughout your journey.

Through this exercise, you'll have the opportunity not only to reflect on your own leadership traits but also to appreciate the diversity of leadership styles and qualities that exist among your peers. Leadership isn't one-size-fits-all, and this activity should provide a visual and introspective exploration of that concept.

Here's a more comprehensive list of leadership traits

Intelligence: The ability to process information, understand complex situations, and devise effective solutions.
Determination: A strong will and persistence in the face of challenges.
Self-confidence: Believing in one's abilities and decisions, even when faced with skepticism or opposition.
Charisma: A natural magnetic personality that draws people in and inspires loyalty.

Adaptability: Flexibility in adjusting to changing circumstances or new information.

Courage: Facing challenges head-on and making difficult decisions even in the presence of fear.

Integrity: Maintaining honesty and consistent moral values.

Sensitivity: Recognizing and respecting the emotions and needs of others.

Energy/Drive: Possessing a high level of stamina and passion towards achieving goals.

Initiative: Taking action proactively without always being directed.

Enthusiasm: Displaying genuine passion and excitement about one's work or cause.

Assertiveness: Clearly expressing one's opinions or desires while respecting others.

Decisiveness: Making clear, timely, and firm decisions.

Empathy: Understanding and sharing the feelings of another.

Creativity: Thinking outside the box and bringing innovative solutions to the table.

Emotional Stability: Maintaining composure and clarity of thought during stressful situations.

Technical/Specialized Knowledge: Possessing expertise in a particular area related to the leadership role.

Tactfulness: Handling situations with care, ensuring feelings and emotions are considered.

Visionary: Being able to see the bigger picture and guide others towards a future goal.

Authenticity: Being genuine and true to oneself and values.

Remember, no leader possesses all of these traits in equal measure. Leadership is about leveraging one's unique combination of these traits, along with skills and experiences, to effectively guide and influence others.

Chapter 2: Modern Approaches to Leadership

In the ever-shifting landscape of leadership research and practice, the evolution from classical to modern approaches marks a significant pivot in how we perceive and understand leadership. While the classical theories provided a foundational understanding of leadership anchored in traits, behaviors, and situational dynamics, the modern era ushered in a deeper, more nuanced exploration of the leader-follower relationship and the very essence of leadership itself.

The modern approaches delve into the complexities of human interactions, motivations, and aspirations within the leadership dynamic. From the transformative energy of transformational leadership to the service-oriented ethos of servant leadership; from the genuine and self-aware principles of authentic leadership to the shared responsibilities highlighted in distributed leadership; and the clear distinctions emphasized in transactional leadership—each of these modern theories offers a unique perspective on leadership, tailored to the multifaceted demands of contemporary society.

These theories not only challenge leaders to refine their skills and adapt to varied contexts but also encourage a profound understanding of oneself and the broader community. As we navigate through the modern approaches, we'll uncover the intricate layers of leadership, emphasizing the significance of connection, authenticity, and shared purpose in today's fast-paced, interconnected world.

Transformational Leadership

Emerging prominently in the latter half of the 20th century, transformational leadership represents a shift in how leadership was understood. This approach centers around leaders who inspire and motivate their followers to exceed their own expectations, pushing boundaries and achieving more than they previously thought possible.

Transformational leaders are visionaries at heart. They have the uncanny ability to craft and share a compelling picture of the future, one that deeply resonates with their followers. This isn't just about setting goals; it's about creating an enticing vision of a brighter future that garners excitement and dedication.

Central to this leadership style is the encouragement of creativity and innovation. Transformational leaders are not content with the status quo. They challenge it, urging their teams to think creatively and approach problems from fresh perspectives. They also understand the importance of recognizing the unique strengths and challenges of each individual within their team. By acting as mentors and coaches, they create an environment where each member feels valued, heard, and understood.

The charisma of transformational leaders is palpable. They possess an innate ability to instill passion and enthusiasm in their teams. Their energy and conviction in their vision become contagious, motivating their followers to join a cause that's greater than any individual aspiration.

The potency of transformational leadership lies in its capability to align the group's values and goals, driving performance and instigating meaningful change. Followers of transformational leaders typically display higher levels of satisfaction, commitment to the organization, and overall performance. In environments demanding adaptability and forward-thinking, this leadership style shines.

Transformational leadership is not without its challenges. It demands a considerable emotional and intellectual commitment from leaders. There's also a balance to strike—between being genuinely inspirational and veering into the realm of the overly idealistic. Hence, it's crucial for leaders of this style to keep their visions grounded in reality while still striving for the exceptional.

In an era marked by swift technological advancements and changing global dynamics, transformational leadership stands poised to guide organizations towards sustained growth and profound impact.

The Psychology of Transformational Leadership

At its core, transformational leadership delves into the deeper layers of human psychology, tapping into both cognitive and emotional processes to inspire followers to transcend their individual ambitions and work towards a collective goal. Unpacking this intricate dance between leaders and followers necessitates a closer look at the psychological mechanisms that underpin this leadership style.

1. Self-Actualization and Maslow's Hierarchy of Needs

One of the foundational psychological theories relevant to transformational leadership is Maslow's hierarchy of needs. At the pinnacle of this pyramid lies self-actualization, representing the realization of an individual's potential. Transformational leaders are adept at helping their followers climb this hierarchy, particularly by addressing esteem needs and guiding them towards self-actualization. By fostering an environment where individuals feel valued and encouraged to grow, these leaders aid in the personal and professional development of their team.

2. Social Identity and Group Cohesion

The transformational leader often cultivates a strong sense of belonging and identity among their followers. By framing challenges and objectives in terms of shared goals and a united purpose, they reinforce the social identity of the group. This enhanced group cohesion not only bolsters teamwork but also fortifies loyalty and commitment to the collective cause.

3. Emotional Resonance and Mirror Neurons

Recent neurological research has highlighted the existence of mirror neurons, cells in the brain that activate both when an action is performed and when it's observed. These neurons are believed to be the foundation of empathy. Transformational leaders, with their charismatic and empathetic nature, resonate emotionally with their followers. This resonance likely taps into the functioning of mirror neurons, allowing leaders and followers to align their emotions and motivations.

4. Cognitive Reframing and Perspective Shifts

Transformational leaders are masters of cognitive reframing. They challenge existing mental models and narratives, encouraging their followers to view challenges as opportunities and obstacles as growth points. This reframing instills a growth mindset among followers, fostering resilience, adaptability, and a penchant for continuous learning.

5. The Role of Dopamine in Motivation

Dopamine, a neurotransmitter, plays a pivotal role in our reward system and is intrinsically linked to motivation. The compelling vision and positive reinforcement provided by transformational leaders can spur the release of dopamine in followers, thereby heightening motivation and engagement.

6. Secure Attachment and Trust-building

Drawing from attachment theory, transformational leaders often cultivate secure attachments with their followers. By being consistently responsive, understanding, and supportive, they build an atmosphere of trust. This secure base allows followers to take risks, innovate, and voice their opinions without fear of reprisal.

The effectiveness of transformational leadership is deeply anchored in its alignment with fundamental psychological processes. By understanding and leveraging these processes, transformational leaders not only guide their teams towards success but also foster environments where individuals thrive, both personally and professionally.

Transactional Leadership

Transactional leadership, rooted in its namesake, revolves around the principle of transactions or exchanges between leaders and followers. Hailing from traditional management practices, this leadership style emphasizes the system of rewards and penalties to regulate performance. Unlike the vision-centric approach of transformational leadership, transactional leadership is about maintaining order and consistency through a methodical approach.

Delving into the psychological nuances of transactional leadership reveals several key attributes. Firstly, the emphasis on clear expectations and structure speaks to the cognitive preference humans have for clarity. When followers are crystal clear about their roles, expected outcomes, and the rewards or penalties tied to those expectations, it alleviates ambiguity. This transparency, in turn, aligns with our inherent psychological need for stability and predictability.

The reward system central to transactional leadership borrows heavily from behaviorism's principles, particularly operant conditioning. In essence, behaviors followed by positive feedback (like rewards) are more likely to recur, while those that invite negative consequences are likely to be avoided. Through these defined contingencies, transactional leaders use the power of reinforcement to mold desired behaviors.

Another defining feature of this leadership style is the clear demarcation of accountability and responsibility. With roles and consequences well-defined, followers often feel a heightened sense of responsibility for their assigned tasks. This direct accountability can, psychologically, increase an individual's commitment and drive to see tasks through to completion.

However, transactional leadership's strong emphasis on external motivators presents both its strength and limitation. While such leadership can effectively drive immediate results, it leans heavily on external rewards and punishments. This might overlook the profound impact of intrinsic motivation, the internal drive that encourages individuals to act out of genuine interest or personal values, often resulting in a deeper and more lasting commitment.

Connecting back to foundational psychological theories like Maslow's hierarchy of needs, transactional leadership caters primarily to the lower tier needs such as safety and physiological well-being. By ensuring consistent rewards for work and a system to correct deviations, it addresses these basic human needs.

Transactional leadership is characterized by its continuous monitoring of performance and consistent feedback loops. While on one hand, this provides opportunities for real-time course corrections, on the other, it might sometimes edge into what feels like micromanagement, potentially suppressing creativity and individual initiative.

Transactional leadership, with its structured and clear modus operandi, can be particularly effective in situations requiring quick compliance or short-term results. However, for environments needing innovation, intrinsic motivation, or a long-term vision, other leadership styles might be more apt.

The Psychology of Transactional Leadership

Transactional leadership is deeply rooted in the principles of B.F. Skinner's operant conditioning. This approach ensures that followers align their behaviors to set norms and guidelines by establishing a direct link between task completion and the subsequent rewards or penalties. By employing rewards for positive behavior and punishments for negative actions, transactional leaders reinforce the likelihood of desired behaviors recurring, while dissuading undesirable ones.

This leadership style also speaks to the human need for structure and predictability. Ambiguity can induce stress and anxiety, whereas clear directives and expectations reduce feelings of uncertainty. Transactional leadership provides this clarity by outlining specific roles, responsibilities, and expected outcomes, catering to our cognitive preference for well-defined structures.

At its core, transactional leadership is driven by extrinsic motivators, which are rewards and punishments from external sources. While these can be effective in the short term, they may not be as sustainable as intrinsic motivators, such as personal interest or values. This reliance on external motivators can sometimes limit the potential for higher levels of creativity and engagement.

Reflecting on Maslow's hierarchy of needs, transactional leadership often addresses the lower levels, ensuring security, stability, and predictability. This focus, while essential, can sometimes overlook the higher-order needs of individuals, such as growth, belonging, and purpose.

The theory of cognitive dissonance, introduced by Leon Festinger, offers another perspective on transactional leadership. When followers recognize the tangible outcomes tied to their tasks, they might adjust their behaviors to align with the anticipated rewards, sidestepping the discomfort of any inconsistency between their actions and expected results.

The regular monitoring and feedback inherent to transactional leadership can be linked to the Zeigarnik effect, which posits that individuals tend to remember uncompleted tasks more than completed ones. The consistent feedback ensures that tasks are brought to closure, capitalizing on this cognitive inclination.

While transactional leadership taps into fundamental human cognitive processes and motivational systems, it's crucial to recognize its limitations, especially in environments that require more innovation, autonomy, and long-term commitment.

Servant Leadership

Servant leadership, a term popularized by Robert K. Greenleaf in the 1970s, diverges from traditional leadership ideologies. Instead of prioritizing the leader's desires or the organization's goals above all else, servant leadership places the needs of the followers front and center. The leader's primary role becomes one of service, ensuring that team members' needs are met and that they're empowered to perform to the best of their abilities.

Psychologically speaking, servant leadership aligns with several fundamental human needs and cognitive processes. At its heart, this leadership style recognizes the inherent value in every individual and seeks to elevate and celebrate it. By doing so, servant leaders tap into the basic human need for validation, belonging, and purpose.

Drawing parallels to Maslow's hierarchy of needs, servant leadership doesn't just address the lower-order needs of safety and security but also emphasizes the higher-order needs. By creating an environment where followers feel valued, supported, and empowered, servant leaders cultivate a space where individuals can pursue self-actualization.

The tenets of servant leadership also resonate with Carl Rogers' person-centered theory in psychology. By providing a non-judgmental, empathetic, and genuine environment, servant leaders create a climate of unconditional positive regard, allowing followers to thrive. In such an atmosphere, individuals feel more accepted, understood, and free to be themselves, which can lead to higher levels of intrinsic motivation, creativity, and innovation.

Another psychological cornerstone of servant leadership is empathy. Empathy, the ability to understand and share the feelings of another, is pivotal in this leadership approach. Research in neuroscience has highlighted the presence of mirror neurons, cells in the brain that fire both when an individual acts and when they observe the same action performed by someone else. This neural mirroring enables individuals to "feel" the emotions of others, laying the foundation for empathy. Servant leaders, with their heightened sense of empathy, can better discern the needs of their followers, leading to more tailored support and guidance.

Servant leadership echoes the principles of positive psychology, which focuses on strengths, virtues, and factors that contribute to a fulfilling life. By nurturing strengths, fostering community, and promoting well-being, servant leaders align closely with the objectives of positive psychology.

Servant leadership, with its emphasis on empathy, growth, and community, draws from a rich tapestry of psychological principles and theories. Its forward-thinking and human-centered approach make it a powerful tool in modern organizational settings, especially in environments that value collaboration, long-term growth, and holistic well-being.

The Psychology of Servant Leadership

Diving deeper into the psychological nuances of servant leadership reveals its interwoven principles with multiple layers of human cognition, motivation, and social interaction.

Drawing from John Bowlby's attachment theory, the supportive and caring nature of servant leadership can create a secure base for followers. This "secure attachment" in the professional realm can mirror the child-caregiver bond seen in early development. Just as a securely attached child feels emboldened to explore their environment and return to their caregiver for support, employees under a servant leader enjoy a similar confidence in taking risks, backed by the knowledge of having steadfast support.

In terms of intrinsic motivation, rooted in Deci and Ryan's Self-Determination Theory, it thrives when three core needs are met: autonomy, competence, and relatedness. Servant leadership naturally caters to these needs. Leaders empower followers, granting them decision-making freedom, thereby addressing the need for autonomy. By offering resources and training, they enhance competence. And, through their genuine care and commitment, they foster a profound sense of relatedness.

Considering the Social Identity Theory, individuals classify themselves and others into various social categories. A servant leader, by prioritizing the needs of their followers, solidifies this 'in-group' sentiment, enhancing the sense of belonging and unity within the team. Such inclusivity can diminish potential conflicts, promoting team cohesion.

Beyond merely recognizing emotions, servant leaders exercise an advanced form of empathy known as "theory of mind." This skill allows leaders to attribute mental states to themselves and others, enabling them to anticipate reactions, grasp underlying motivations, and address latent concerns, thus offering more tailored and effective support.

The concept of the growth mindset, introduced by Carol Dweck, posits that abilities and intelligence can be developed. Servant leaders, with their emphasis on personal development and continuous learning, naturally cultivate this mindset in their followers. They shape an environment where challenges transform into opportunities and failures become steppingstones for growth.

At its heart, servant leadership embodies an altruistic approach, genuinely prioritizing the well-being of followers. This genuine care often spurs reciprocity, a social expectation where acts of kindness are reciprocated. Teams led by such leaders frequently showcase heightened collaboration, trust, and mutual support, initiating a positive cycle of goodwill.

By grounding their leadership in these profound psychological principles, servant leaders not only ensure the optimal functioning and well-being of their followers but also lay the foundation for sustained organizational success. The intricate psychological underpinnings of servant leadership amplify its potential to mold not just productive teams but also resilient, adaptive, and harmonious organizational cultures.

Authentic Leadership

The call for more genuine and transparent leaders has given rise to the concept of authentic leadership. Rooted in authenticity, this leadership style emphasizes a consistent alignment between a leader's values, beliefs, desires, and actions. Authentic leaders prioritize self-awareness, act with integrity, and maintain open and honest relationships with their followers.

One of the defining features of authentic leadership is self-awareness. Authentic leaders possess a profound understanding of their own strengths, weaknesses, values, and emotions. This introspective quality allows them to remain true to themselves, even when faced with challenging decisions. They recognize their own imperfections, learning from their mistakes and continually striving for personal growth.

Operating with an unwavering internal moral compass, authentic leaders prioritize integrity in every action. Their decisions and actions align seamlessly with their deeply held values and beliefs. They don't bend to external pressures or alter their stance to appease others. Instead, they make decisions that they believe are right, fostering trust and respect among their followers.

Another hallmark of authentic leadership is relational transparency. Authentic leaders are open and genuine in their interactions, fostering environments where open communication and feedback are encouraged. They don't hide behind facades or wear masks to suit different audiences. Instead, they express their true thoughts and feelings, even if they reveal vulnerability.

From a psychological perspective, the transparency and consistency displayed by authentic leaders can lead to a myriad of positive outcomes. For followers, the consistent and genuine nature of authentic leaders often results in increased trust. This trust can foster improved job satisfaction, commitment, and emotional well-being. Additionally, in an age where authenticity is highly sought after, organizations led by authentic leaders tend to attract and retain top talent, cultivate ethical workplaces, and demonstrate increased adaptability in the face of change.

Authentic leadership represents a return to the foundational principles of leadership: leading with integrity, honesty, and genuineness. In a complex and ever-evolving world, leaders who remain true to themselves and act with unwavering authenticity serve as beacons of stability and trustworthiness, guiding their organizations toward success with grace and resilience.

The Psychology of Authentic Leadership

From a psychological standpoint, the underpinnings of authentic leadership are deeply intertwined with several key facets. Authentic leaders are deeply introspective, possessing a clear understanding of their strengths, weaknesses, motivations, and emotions. This heightened self-awareness is akin to the concept of metacognition—a term that describes one's ability to think about one's own thinking. By consistently reflecting upon and evaluating their actions and decisions, authentic leaders can align their behavior with their core values, fostering a genuine leadership style that is both consistent and predictable.

Rooted in Kohlberg's stages of moral development, authentic leaders often operate with an internalized moral perspective. They function at the post-conventional level, where morality is defined by internal principles rather than societal norms. This intrinsic moral compass guides them in making decisions that are ethically sound and in the best interests of all stakeholders, even without external validation or reward.

Authentic leaders are open to feedback and actively seek diverse opinions before making decisions. This aspect of authentic leadership is related to the cognitive concept of "decentering," which involves viewing situations from multiple perspectives, thereby reducing the influence of cognitive biases. By taking into account various viewpoints and objectively analyzing information, these leaders make well-informed decisions and encourage a culture of open dialogue.

In terms of relational transparency, authentic leadership intersects with humanistic psychology. Leaders who are relationally transparent show their true selves to others. Expressing their genuine thoughts and feelings, they foster an environment of trust and open communication. This can be likened to Carl Rogers' concept of congruence—where one's self-image aligns with their actions and outer persona. When leaders are congruent, they are perceived as genuine, which establishes stronger interpersonal connections.

In a psychological context, authentic leadership can have profound effects on followers. By modeling genuine behavior, leaders inspire authenticity in their teams. This often results in increased trust, enhanced job satisfaction, and improved well-being among employees. Moreover, the transparent and moral nature of authentic leadership often cultivates organizational environments that are ethically grounded and socially responsible. As authenticity is highly valued in today's age, leaders who embrace these qualities not only elevate their own leadership efficacy but also create a ripple effect of authenticity throughout their organizations, making them more resilient, ethical, and adaptable in a rapidly evolving world.

Distributed Leadership

Distributed leadership, often referred to as shared or collaborative leadership, challenges the traditional hierarchical model of leadership where one individual holds primary responsibility for leading. Instead, it posits that leadership is a collective process, spread among individuals within an organization. This approach underscores that leadership is not confined to designated roles or positions but emerges through interactions and relationships among various stakeholders.

In a distributed leadership framework, leadership is seen as an activity rather than a title. It's less about the formal authority one wields and more about the collaborative processes, tasks, and functions that are spread across people. Essentially, it acknowledges that expertise, influence, and leadership capabilities can exist anywhere within an organization.

This leadership model is rooted in the belief that all members of an organization possess unique talents, experiences, and perspectives that can be harnessed for the greater good. By decentralizing leadership, distributed leadership fosters a culture of empowerment, where individuals feel valued and have a sense of ownership in the organization's success.

The Psychology of Distributed Leadership

From a psychological standpoint, distributed leadership taps into the intrinsic motivation of individuals. When members feel they have a voice and are trusted with responsibilities, their commitment, job satisfaction, and sense of purpose often surge. There's also a collective sense of accountability, as leadership is viewed as a shared endeavor.

Distributed leadership aligns well with the demands of the modern, interconnected, and rapidly changing work environments. As organizations become more complex, the challenges they face often require diverse expertise and collaborative solutions. A distributed leadership approach can capitalize on the collective intelligence and agility of its members, ensuring that decisions and strategies are informed by a rich tapestry of insights.

It's worth noting that while distributed leadership offers numerous advantages, its implementation requires a cultural shift. Organizations must be prepared to move away from deeply entrenched hierarchies, fostering an environment of trust, open communication, and collaboration. Leaders, in this context, play a crucial role in facilitating, coordinating, and nurturing the distribution of leadership tasks and functions.

Distributed leadership offers a fresh, dynamic perspective on leadership, one that resonates with the collaborative spirit of contemporary organizations. It underscores the idea that leadership is not a solitary endeavor, but a collective symphony of voices working harmoniously towards shared goals.

Distributed leadership emerges from a profound understanding of human psychology and group dynamics. It's not merely an administrative or managerial approach but is rooted deeply in how people perceive themselves within a group, their intrinsic motivations, and the nature of collaborative relationships.

The concept challenges traditional beliefs about power dynamics and authority. Traditional hierarchical structures are based on a top-down model, where power is concentrated at the top. In contrast, distributed leadership operates on the premise that power, influence, and decision-making capabilities can be found throughout an organization. This democratization of power aligns with human beings' inherent desire for autonomy and self-determination, as posited by Self-Determination Theory. When individuals feel a sense of ownership and agency in their roles, they are more likely to be intrinsically motivated, leading to enhanced commitment and performance.

Another psychological cornerstone of distributed leadership is the social constructivist perspective. Leadership, in this model, is seen as a socially constructed phenomenon that arises from interactions within a group. It's less about individual prowess and more about collective capabilities. This perspective aligns with Vygotsky's theory that social interaction plays a fundamental role in cognitive development. Similarly, in distributed leadership, leadership capabilities are honed and refined through continuous interactions, feedback, and collaboration.

The distributed leadership model acknowledges the complex, multifaceted nature of human intelligence and capability. Howard Gardner's theory of multiple intelligences suggests that intelligence is not monolithic but exists in various forms, such as linguistic, logical-mathematical, spatial, and interpersonal, to name a few. Distributed leadership taps into this diversity of intelligences by recognizing and harnessing the unique strengths and capabilities present throughout an organization.

From a social psychology perspective, distributed leadership fosters a strong sense of group cohesion and collective identity. When leadership is seen as a shared endeavor, individuals are more likely to perceive themselves as integral parts of a larger whole. This sense of belongingness, as highlighted in Maslow's hierarchy of needs, is fundamental to human well-being. Furthermore, when individuals identify strongly with their groups, they are more inclined to prioritize group goals over individual agendas, leading to aligned efforts and synergistic outcomes.

Distributed leadership addresses the cognitive biases and limitations inherent in single-leader models. As Daniel Kahneman's work on cognitive biases highlights, individual decision-making can often be clouded by various biases, leading to suboptimal outcomes. A distributed leadership model, by involving diverse perspectives and voices, can serve as a corrective mechanism, ensuring decisions are more balanced, holistic, and well-informed. The distributed leadership model draws from various psychological theories and principles, offering a comprehensive, human-centric approach to leadership that resonates with the intrinsic needs, motivations, and capacities of individuals within collaborative settings.

While this exploration delves deep into some specific leadership models, it's essential to acknowledge the vast landscape of leadership theories that exist. Leadership, as a field of study, has evolved over centuries, giving rise to numerous frameworks, models, and paradigms. Each brings unique insights and perspectives on how individuals can effectively guide, influence, and inspire others.

From charismatic leadership, which emphasizes the magnetic allure of leaders, to ethical leadership that underscores the importance of moral integrity, and from adaptive leadership, which focuses on navigating change, to cross-cultural leadership that emphasizes the nuances of leading in diverse cultural contexts—there is a wealth of knowledge and understanding out there. There's also the notion of quiet leadership, which champions the idea that one doesn't need to be boisterous or dominant to be an effective leader.

Each of these models, and many others not mentioned here, offer valuable lessons and insights. While our focus in this exploration is narrowed to certain frameworks, it's crucial for readers and aspiring leaders to understand that the world of leadership is vast and multifaceted. Exploring various models and theories can provide a richer, more holistic understanding of leadership, allowing individuals to adapt and tailor their approach depending on the context, the people involved, and the challenges faced.

Exercise 2: for Authentic Leadership: "The Authenticity Reflection Circle"

Objective: Dive deep into the principles of authentic leadership, enabling you to reflect on your own experiences and gain insights into your authentic leadership journey.

Activity: Authenticity Story Swap

Materials Needed:
- ☐ Pen and a notepad or journal
- ☐ A timer or stopwatch
- ☐ A comfortable seating area, preferably arranged in a circle

Instructions:

Understanding Authentic Leadership: Let's begin with a quick chat about authentic leadership – see also section on Authentic Leadership in this chapter. It's all about being genuine, self-aware, and transparent. As an authentic leader, you'll lead with heart, show vulnerability when needed, and stay committed to long-term, value-based leadership.

Personal Reflection:
a. Take about 10 minutes to think about a time when you felt you were truly being your authentic self. Maybe it was when you stood up for something you believed in, faced a personal challenge head-on, or made a decision rooted deeply in your core values.
b. Write down this experience, making a note of what this incident taught you about your unique leadership style.

Sharing in the Authenticity Circle:
a. Once you've penned down your thoughts, we'll go around the circle, and each of you will get a chance to share your story.

b. After each person shares, there will be a brief 2–3-minute window for others to ask questions or share their takeaways from the story.

c. We'll continue this process until everyone has shared their story. Please be mindful of time to ensure everyone gets their turn.

Reflecting Together: After all stories are shared, let's discuss as a group. What common themes or feelings did you notice? How can these personal moments shape our journey towards becoming authentic leaders?

Debrief: To wrap things up, we'll reflect on the value of authentic leadership. Remember, in a world where it's easy to be influenced by external factors, staying true to yourself and leading with genuine intent is invaluable. It builds trust, nurtures relationships, and paves the way for meaningful leadership.

Through this exercise, you'll not only introspect on your authentic leadership journey but also hear diverse experiences from your peers. Listening and sharing in such a supportive setting will allow you to appreciate the power and importance of authenticity in leadership.

Chapter 3: Leadership and Personality

The realm of leadership is vast, multifaceted, and intricately woven with threads of numerous disciplines. Yet, among the myriad aspects that shape leadership dynamics, the influence of personality stands out as both foundational and transformative. This relationship between leadership and personality is reminiscent of a dance where the rhythm, pace, and grace of every move is dictated by the inherent nature of the dancer. Just as every dancer brings their unique flair to a performance, every leader's personality imparts a distinct touch to their leadership style.

Our personality, an intricate tapestry woven from our experiences, genetic makeup, upbringing, and societal influences, serves as the lens through which we perceive, interact with, and shape the world around us. It is, in many ways, the core of our being, influencing our decisions, reactions, aspirations, and relationships. When this personal realm intersects with the domain of leadership, the results can be profound, varied, and at times, unexpected.

In this chapter, we journey into the heart of this convergence, unraveling the ways in which distinct personality aspects impact leadership dynamics. Beginning with the Big Five Personality Traits, we will explore the broad dimensions of human personality and their repercussions in leadership scenarios. As we move deeper, the realm of Emotional Intelligence beckons, shedding light on the emotional underpinnings that can make or break leadership endeavors. Yet, every story has its shadows, and our exploration would be incomplete without a foray into the darker facets of personality, as epitomized by the Dark Triad Traits and their complex relationship with leadership.

As you immerse yourself in this exploration, you'll be prompted to reflect, introspect, and perhaps even recalibrate aspects of your leadership approach. The intersection of leadership and personality is not just academic; it's deeply personal. By understanding the myriad ways in which our intrinsic nature influences our leadership journey, we pave the way for more conscious, adaptive, and impactful leadership.

The Big Five Personality Traits

The Big Five Personality Traits, often referred to as the Five Factor Model, comprises five broad dimensions of personality that have been consistently identified in various cultures and settings. These are Openness to Experience, Conscientiousness, Extraversion, Agreeableness, and Neuroticism (often termed Emotional Stability in a positive framing). Each of these traits provides a spectrum along which individual personalities can be mapped, offering a holistic overview of one's inherent tendencies.

Openness to Experience is one of the five major dimensions of personality often highlighted in the Big Five personality model. People with a high degree of this trait tend to be imaginative, curious, and have a pronounced eagerness to explore novel ideas and experiences. Such individuals possess a broader and more differentiated cognitive palette than those less open, and they perceive the world with a sense of novelty, possibility, and wonder.

Curiosity is a standout feature of this trait. Highly curious individuals are avid learners, constantly probing deeper into topics, asking more questions, and seeking out the underlying principles or broader contexts. Their creativity extends beyond just artistic endeavors. Leaders with a robust sense of openness frequently think outside the conventional frameworks, identifying unique solutions to challenges and innovating in areas that might surprise many. Their love for novel experiences means they don't recoil from the unfamiliar. Be it a fresh cultural insight, a new strategy, or a different perspective on a longstanding issue, they are ready to embrace change.

When it comes to leadership, those with a strong inclination towards openness can be game changers for organizations. Such leaders often form the backbone of organizational innovation. They are not content with merely accepting things as they are; they actively challenge the status quo in a bid to improve and advance. They also have a penchant for valuing and actively seeking input from a diverse range of sources, recognizing that the most effective solutions are often the result of considering a multitude of perspectives. Moreover, under their guidance, a culture emerges where learning becomes a continuous journey. They inspire their teams and peers to relentlessly pursue new knowledge, whether through formal training sessions or individual quests for understanding.

Strengths, when not balanced, can sometimes veer into the territory of weaknesses. Leaders with a high degree of openness need to be wary of certain pitfalls. The constant allure of the new and different might divert their attention from the primary mission, causing a scattering of energy and resources. Established norms and practices in any organization often have deep-rooted reasons for their existence. While it's commendable to seek out new approaches, leaders must ensure they have valid reasons for deviating from established norms. There's also the danger of constantly questing for novelty, which can lead to overthinking situations, thereby causing delays in decision-making.

Conscientiousness, a crucial facet of the Big Five personality model, encompasses traits associated with reliability, organization, and systematic approaches. Individuals with high levels of conscientiousness are not just responsible; they take immense pride in their organizational skills and their ability to carry out tasks with accuracy.

A leader steeped in conscientiousness often emerges as a beacon of dependability within an organization. When they commit, colleagues and team members trust that the task will not only be initiated but will also see a meticulous conclusion. This consistency in execution builds trust, ensuring everyone involved feels confident about the project's direction and outcome. Their methodical approach is palpable. They don't merely begin tasks; they proceed with clarity and a well-laid plan, addressing every detail and ensuring thoroughness at every stage. This meticulousness also translates into how they uphold standards within the organization. For them, processes exist for a reason, ensuring consistency, minimizing mistakes, and achieving dependable outcomes.

As with all personality traits, conscientiousness, when magnified or in specific contexts, can pose challenges. Leaders abundant in this trait may excel in stable environments where tasks can be planned and executed systematically. Yet, in the face of rapid changes, which are commonplace in today's dynamic business world, they may find it daunting to adapt swiftly. Their inherent leaning towards well-laid plans might make spontaneous adjustments seem alien, if not entirely counterintuitive. Further, while processes are undeniably vital for ensuring consistency, an excessive dependence on them can curtail innovation and nimbleness. There's the potential danger that these leaders might become excessively process-driven, overlooking solutions that don't fit within their familiar frameworks. Another aspect of their detail-oriented nature, which is often a strength, might sometimes lead them into the trap of overthinking. Their drive for perfection in every detail might delay pivotal decisions or overshadow the overarching goal.

Extraversion is a vibrant component of the Big Five personality model, typified by an unmistakable outward energy and zest for life. Those who exude this trait seem to have an inexhaustible reservoir of enthusiasm, drawing from it to engage with the world around them actively.

Leaders who embody extraversion often stand out in a crowd, not just because they seek the limelight, but because they naturally attract it. Their innate ability to connect with others allows them to weave extensive networks with ease. Such leaders don't merely exchange business cards; they form lasting impressions, turning brief interactions into meaningful connections.

The extraverted leader's energy doesn't remain confined to them. It ripples outward, galvanizing teams and inspiring collective enthusiasm. In roles that demand public interactions – be it presentations, negotiations, or team meetings – these leaders don't just perform; they thrive. They harness their natural charisma to not only command attention but also to steer that attention towards shared goals. When morale dips or direction is needed, the extraverted leader's buoyant spirit can act as a beacon, uplifting team spirits and aligning everyone towards a common objective.

Every strength, when not balanced, can cast a shadow. The extraverted leader's thirst for external stimuli, their drive to be in the midst of action, might at times come at the expense of quieter, introspective moments. Leadership, as much as it demands action, also requires periods of reflection, where strategies are contemplated, and future paths charted. There's a risk that the constant external engagement might drown out the softer, internal voice that beckons them to pause, think, and introspect.

Openness to Experience

Individuals scoring high on this trait are often characterized by their curiosity, creativity, and a penchant for novel experiences. In a leadership context, such individuals are more likely to embrace innovative approaches, encourage out-of-the-box thinking, and be receptive to diverse viewpoints. Their leadership style might foster an environment of continuous learning and exploration. On the flip side, excessive openness might lead to a lack of focus or a tendency to deviate from established norms without adequate reason.

Conscientiousness

Leaders high in conscientiousness are typically methodical, organized, and dependable. They value consistency, diligence, and are driven by a sense of duty. Such leaders can be the backbone of organizations, ensuring projects are seen to completion and standards are maintained. However, an overly conscientious leader might struggle with flexibility and could be resistant to adapting to changing scenarios.

Extraversion

Extraverted leaders are outgoing, energetic, and thrive in social situations. Their charisma often draws people to them, making them effective in roles that require networking, team motivation, and public speaking. These leaders are adept at energizing their teams and rallying them towards a common goal. Yet, their zest for external stimulation might sometimes overshadow the need for introspection or deep, focused work.

Agreeableness

Leaders scoring high in agreeableness are compassionate, cooperative, and value harmonious relationships. Their empathetic nature often makes them approachable, fostering a culture of trust and mutual respect. While these traits are commendable, an excessively agreeable leader might face challenges in situations that demand tough decision-making or confrontation.

Neuroticism (Emotional Stability)

This trait pertains to the degree to which individuals experience negative emotions such as anxiety, anger, or depression. Leaders with low levels of neuroticism (or high emotional stability) tend to be calm under pressure, resilient in the face of challenges, and less likely to be swayed by emotional turbulence. Conversely, those high in neuroticism might struggle with stress management and might be perceived as less predictable.

Agreeableness is a distinct facet of the Big Five personality model, characterized by a genuine affinity for fostering positive interpersonal relations. Leaders suffused with agreeableness tend to naturally radiate warmth and understanding. Their leadership style isn't dictated by mere protocols or hierarchy; instead, it's driven by a genuine desire to understand, collaborate, and create harmonious work environments.

Such leaders are often the touchstone of empathy within an organization. They have an uncanny ability to sense the pulse of their teams, to understand their joys and concerns, and to respond with compassion. This deep sense of empathy makes them inherently approachable. Colleagues and subordinates don't view them merely as figureheads but as confidantes, fostering a culture where open communication is encouraged, and trust is effortlessly built.

Agreeableness also manifests in a cooperative spirit. These leaders are less likely to be autocratic or domineering. Instead, they believe in collaborative efforts, pooling in diverse perspectives, and making decisions that reflect collective wisdom. Such an inclusive approach can be instrumental in weaving a tight-knit team, where members feel valued and heard.

The very strengths that make agreeable leaders beloved can, at times, also be their Achilles' heel. Their intrinsic desire to maintain harmony and avoid conflict can sometimes become a hindrance. Leadership, by its very nature, requires tough decisions, and not every decision will be met with universal approval. There are times when difficult conversations are necessary, when unpopular decisions need to be made, or when underperformance needs to be addressed. An overemphasis on maintaining accord can make navigating such situations challenging for highly agreeable leaders. There's a risk that they might sidestep crucial issues in the quest to avoid ruffling feathers.

Neuroticism and its more positively framed counterpart, Emotional Stability, offer a lens into the emotional resilience and reactivity of an individual. This dimension, central to the Big Five personality model, gives us insight into how individuals handle stress, challenges, and unexpected turns of events.

Leaders imbued with high emotional stability stand out as rocks amidst tumultuous waters. They exude a calm and balanced demeanor, regardless of the external pressures or challenges they might be facing. Their ability to remain collected isn't merely for their own benefit; it acts as an anchor for the entire team. In chaotic situations, teams often look to their leaders for guidance and reassurance. A leader with a strong sense of emotional stability provides that crucial steadying influence, guiding the team with a clear head and a calm spirit. Their composure in the face of adversity not only aids in making rational decisions but also instills confidence within the team, assuring them that challenges can be surmounted.

Conversely, leaders with heightened neuroticism navigate the world of leadership with a different set of challenges. Their heightened emotional reactivity means that stresses, be they big or small, might elicit more profound emotional responses. Such leaders may find themselves caught in a constant flux of emotions, from anxiety to irritability, especially when situations don't unfold as anticipated. While a degree of emotional sensitivity can be advantageous, making leaders more attuned to the nuances of their environment and team, excessive neuroticism can make consistent stress management a challenge. This can, over time, translate to a perceived unpredictability in leadership style. Teams might find it hard to gauge their leader's reactions or might feel apprehensive about bringing bad news or challenges to their attention.

Appreciating the nuances of these traits is pivotal for leaders. Not as a prescriptive measure, but as a mirror that reflects inherent tendencies, enabling them to harness their strengths and be cognizant of areas requiring attention. Leadership, after all, is not about fitting into a mold but about understanding oneself, adapting to contexts, and guiding teams with authenticity and insight.

The intricate dance between these personality traits and leadership underscores the importance of self-awareness. While no particular combination of traits guarantees successful leadership, understanding one's predispositions can empower leaders to leverage their strengths and be mindful of potential areas for growth. Moreover, it's essential to recognize that leadership effectiveness isn't solely dependent on individual traits but also on how these traits align with the specific context, team dynamics, and organizational culture in which a leader operates.

Emotional Intelligence

Emotional Intelligence (EI) is more than just a buzzword in the leadership lexicon; it's a cornerstone of effective leadership in the modern era. Rooted deeply in the interplay of personal and social competencies, EI provides leaders with the ability to recognize, comprehend, and manage their emotions while also understanding and influencing the emotions of those around them.

The first and most fundamental component of EI is self-awareness. A leader with a heightened sense of self-awareness understands their emotional triggers, strengths, and areas of growth. This introspective insight enables them to respond to challenging situations with clarity and discernment instead of reacting impulsively.

Building upon self-awareness is self-regulation. Leaders who can regulate their emotions can navigate the turbulent waters of conflict, stress, and high-pressure decisions without being swayed unduly by their immediate emotions. By maintaining calm and demonstrating emotional resilience, they set a positive example for their team, creating an environment of stability and trust.

Motivation, another facet of EI, moves beyond mere external rewards or recognitions. Leaders with intrinsic motivation are driven by a deeper purpose and a genuine passion for their work. This inner drive is infectious, inspiring teams to pursue shared objectives with a sense of commitment and enthusiasm.

There's empathy, the ability to genuinely understand and share the feelings of another. Empathetic leaders are attuned to the subtle emotional undercurrents within their teams. They can gauge the mood, anticipate concerns, and address potential issues before they escalate. Such leaders create a culture where team members feel heard, valued, and understood.

Social skills in EI encompass a leader's ability to manage interpersonal relationships judiciously and empathetically. This is where the intricate dance of communication, conflict resolution, and collaboration comes into play. Leaders with refined social skills can foster strong relationships, build cohesive teams, and steer collective energy towards common goals.

In the diverse and dynamic landscape of leadership, Emotional Intelligence is not merely an asset but a necessity. It equips leaders to form genuine connections, navigate challenges with grace, and cultivate an environment where teams can thrive both professionally and personally.

Emotional intelligence, at its core, is intertwined with various psychological constructs, giving leaders an edge in understanding and navigating the intricate web of human interactions and responses within an organizational setting.

Emotional intelligence emerges from the understanding that our emotions are not mere reactions but informative signals about our internal state and external circumstances. The nuances of emotional responses are rooted in both evolutionary adaptations and personal experiences. For instance, fear might have once signaled a threat in our environment, prompting a fight or flight response. In the modern world, while the threats have changed— like a looming deadline or an important presentation—the emotional reaction remains deeply ingrained in our psyche.

Leaders with heightened emotional intelligence possess an innate ability to decode these emotional responses, not only in themselves but also in their teams. They recognize that behind every emotion is a plethora of information about an individual's current state of mind, their preferences, values, and even their underlying motivations. Such leaders don't merely react to emotions; they interpret and act upon them in a way that is both insightful and constructive.

The realm of emotional intelligence extends into cognitive processes. Emotions and cognition are intrinsically linked. For instance, a leader's decision-making process is not solely based on logic or information at hand. It's often influenced by their emotional state. Understanding this interplay, emotionally intelligent leaders are more apt at mitigating cognitive biases that emotions might introduce, ensuring decisions are well-rounded and considerate of both logical and emotional facets.

Empathy, a cornerstone of emotional intelligence, is deeply rooted in our neurobiology. Neuroscientists have identified 'mirror neurons' in our brains that help us resonate with others' feelings.

Leaders with a refined sense of empathy tap into this neural network, allowing them to 'feel' what their team feels. This mirroring process enables leaders to address concerns, mediate conflicts, and create an inclusive environment where every member feels understood and valued.

At a deeper psychological level, emotional intelligence also ties into our self-concept and self-worth. Leaders who are emotionally intelligent often have a secure sense of self. They are neither overly critical nor unrealistically optimistic about their abilities and worth. This balanced self-view equips them to handle feedback, face failures, and manage successes with grace and humility.

Emotional intelligence, when viewed through the lens of psychology, presents itself as a harmonious blend of evolutionary adaptations, cognitive processes, neurobiology, and personal experiences. Emotionally intelligent leadership, therefore, is not just about understanding feelings; it's about delving deep into the psyche to foster connections, inspire trust, and lead with authenticity and insight.

Dark Triad Traits in Leadership

While traits like Emotional Intelligence are often lauded for their positive impact on leadership, it's also essential to explore the more ominous side of personality and its influence on leadership styles. Enter the Dark Triad: a set of three personality traits that, while sometimes beneficial in the short term, can be detrimental in leadership roles over the long haul. The Dark Triad consists of narcissism, Machiavellianism, and psychopathy.

Narcissism in leadership often manifests as a heightened sense of self-importance and a constant need for admiration. Narcissistic leaders may have a grandiose sense of self and believe that they possess unique abilities that others don't. While their confidence can sometimes drive teams forward, their lack of consideration for others and their sensitivity to criticism can create rifts within teams and hinder collaboration.

Machiavellianism is characterized by manipulation and exploitation of others, where the end justifies the means. Leaders with high Machiavellian traits are often strategic and can be adept at navigating organizational politics, but at the expense of ethical considerations. Their focus on personal gain, sometimes at the detriment of others, can erode trust and create a toxic work environment.

Lastly, **psychopathy,** although less common, is particularly concerning in leadership roles. Leaders with psychopathic traits might exhibit a lack of remorse, shallow emotions, and impulsivity. Their risk-taking can sometimes lead to short-term gains, but their inability to form genuine emotional connections and their tendency towards unethical behavior can have severe long-term implications for organizations.

Understanding these dark traits is crucial, not to stereotype or stigmatize, but to be aware of potential pitfalls and challenges in leadership dynamics. While not every leader with these traits will manifest negative behaviors, recognizing the signs can help teams and organizations put checks and balances in place, ensuring a healthy and collaborative work environment.

The study of personality in leadership is vast and multifaceted. From the positive influences of the Big Five and Emotional Intelligence to the challenges posed by the Dark Triad, understanding the intricate interplay of these traits provides a richer, more nuanced view of leadership in various contexts.

From a psychological vantage point, the prevalence of individuals with Dark Triad traits in leadership roles is a fascinating phenomenon. This prevalence can be attributed to a confluence of factors that make such personalities not only ascend the leadership ladder but also, at times, thrive within it:

Charisma and Confidence

One of the hallmarks of Dark Triad traits, especially evident in narcissism, is an unmistakable charisma. These individuals exude a confidence that many find magnetic, and their ability to present themselves assuredly often captivates those around them. In settings where initial impressions matter, such as interviews or electoral campaigns, this charisma becomes a potent tool. It offers them a distinct advantage, positioning them as natural leaders or people who can take charge.

Risk-Taking

The tendency to act impulsively, often associated with psychopathy within the Dark Triad, lends itself to daring decisions. In volatile sectors or unpredictable situations, such audacious decision-making can, on occasion, translate to remarkable successes. This risk affinity can be seen as visionary or groundbreaking, especially when such risks lead to positive outcomes. However, it's essential to recognize the double-edged nature of this trait, as the same risks can lead to significant failures or harms.

Manipulative Skills

Leadership, in many ways, is about influencing others—molding their thoughts, aligning their actions, and steering them towards a collective goal. In this arena, the Machiavellian tendencies of manipulation and strategic maneuvering shine. Individuals with high Machiavellianism, or even pronounced narcissistic traits, possess a knack for shaping scenarios or swaying individuals to fit their narrative or further their objectives.

It's crucial to underscore that the mere presence of these Dark Triad traits doesn't guarantee efficacious or moral leadership. Indeed, many organizations under the helm of such leaders witness heightened internal strife, diminished team spirit, and an environment where unethical practices might become the norm rather than the exception. Therefore, comprehending the psychological intricacies of the Dark Triad within leadership contexts becomes imperative. Such understanding allows organizations to install safeguards, nurturing leadership that is not just effective in its pursuits but also upholds the pillars of ethics and integrity.

Exercise 3: Emotional Intelligence in Leadership: "Navigating Emotions Workshop"

Objective: Delve deep into the facets of emotional intelligence (EI) and understand its profound impact on leadership. By recognizing, interpreting, and responding to emotions, both in yourself and others, you'll enhance your leadership capabilities.

Activity: Emotion Role-Playing

Materials Needed:

Emotion cards: These cards will have different scenarios or situations written on them that evoke specific emotions.
Instructions:

Unpacking Emotional Intelligence: Emotional intelligence consists of five components:
1. Self-awareness: Recognizing your emotions as they occur.
2. Self-regulation: Managing and adapting your emotions depending on the situation.
3. Motivation: Being driven to achieve goals for personal reasons beyond just external rewards.
4. Empathy: Recognizing and understanding the emotions of others.
5. Social skills: Managing relationships and building networks effectively.

Emotion Role-Playing
a. Divide into pairs. Each pair will pick an emotion card which will describe a scenario. One person in the pair will act out the scenario, and the other will attempt to interpret the emotion being displayed.
b. After acting out the scenario, the observer will discuss the emotion they interpreted, how it made them feel, and provide

feedback on how the scenario could be approached using the components of EI.

c. Swap roles and repeat with a new emotion card.

Group Reflection
a. After all pairs have finished role-playing, come back together as a group.
b. Discuss the challenges and revelations you experienced during the role-playing. Was it easy to interpret emotions? How did the feedback from your partner help you understand the importance of EI in leadership?

Emotional Intelligence in Action
a. Reflect on a past situation where emotional intelligence (or a lack thereof) played a key role. How might a stronger grasp of EI have changed the outcome?
b. Share your reflections with the group and discuss strategies to enhance EI in similar future situations.

Debrief: Emotional intelligence isn't just about recognizing emotions; it's about using that awareness to foster stronger relationships, make informed decisions, and lead with empathy and understanding. As you progress in your leadership journey, cultivating EI will be instrumental in navigating complex interpersonal dynamics and fostering a positive and productive environment.

Through this exercise, you'll gain hands-on experience in recognizing and interpreting emotions, using them constructively in leadership scenarios, and understanding the profound impact of emotional intelligence on leadership effectiveness.

Chapter 4: The Social Psychology of Leadership

Leadership, in its essence, isn't just an individual endeavor: it thrives within the intricacies of human interactions and social structures. As we dive deeper into understanding leadership, we cannot overlook the social underpinnings that shape, challenge, and often redefine the pathways of leadership. This chapter, anchored in the rich terrain of social psychology, explores the profound interplay between leadership and the multifaceted dimensions of human social behavior.

At the heart of leadership lie group dynamics. Leaders do not operate in isolation; they are part of teams, organizations, communities, and societies. The manner in which individuals behave within these groups—whether harmoniously converging towards a common goal or conflicting due to disparate interests—profoundly influences leadership approaches and outcomes. But what catalyzes these group behaviors? How do leaders navigate the murky waters of group biases, internal politics, and collective aspirations?

Equally central to the discourse on leadership is the concept of power. Power is not merely about authoritative commands; it's a nuanced tool that can be wielded in myriad ways. The sources from which leaders derive their power, be it from expertise, charisma, or formal positions, significantly shape their influence strategies. Moreover, how leaders exercise this power—whether they employ it judiciously for collective good or misuse it for personal gains—can leave indelible imprints on their leadership legacies.

Leadership's dance with social psychology doesn't end with group dynamics and power alone. We are compelled to delve into concepts like conformity, compliance, and obedience. These elements hold a mirror to society, reflecting how individuals often react to authority and peer pressure. When does a team's adherence to a leader's vision signify alignment, and when does it border on blind obedience? Where does the line blur between constructive conformity and stifling uniformity?

In this chapter, we will journey through the vast corridors of social psychology to unravel these questions and more. We aim to offer a comprehensive lens to view leadership, not just as a solitary pursuit but as a dynamic entity deeply intertwined with the social fabric of human interactions. Through this exploration, we hope to equip readers with insights and tools that enable them to be not just effective leaders, but also conscious navigators of the complex social terrains they tread upon.

Social Psychology

Social psychology can be envisioned as the intricate tapestry of human interaction, one that weaves together the threads of individual thoughts, feelings, and behaviors under the overarching loom of societal presence. It dives deep into the reservoir of human nature, unearthing how our beliefs and actions morph in the company of others, be it through direct interactions, imagined scenarios, or societal norms. As we journey through this chapter, this discipline serves as our compass, guiding us through the societal landscapes that shape leadership dynamics.

Leadership

Leadership, a term often shrouded in grandeur, is at its core a deeply human endeavor. It's the art and science of influencing, an intricate dance of guiding individuals towards a shared horizon. Beyond titles and hierarchies, leadership resonates in the heartbeats of inspiration, the hands that mold visions into realities, and the voices that rise above challenges to rally collective spirits. In the theater of social interactions, leadership is both the script and the performance, constantly evolving in response to the ever-shifting dynamics of human behavior.

The Role of Group Dynamics in Leadership

Leadership does not unfold in a vacuum. It blossoms and evolves within the rich and often unpredictable gardens of group dynamics. While individual competence and vision are indispensable components of effective leadership, it's the larger dance of interpersonal relationships, group cohesion, and shared goals that ultimately determine the trajectory and success of leadership endeavors.

A Symphony of Interactions

The orchestra analogy isn't merely a poetic depiction of group dynamics; it encapsulates the intricate nuances of leadership within a collective setting. In every orchestra, from the deep timbre of cellos to the bright sparkle of flutes and the steady rhythm of percussions, each instrument has its unique voice. Similarly, within any group, diverse personalities echo these musical traits. Some members resonate with the assertiveness of a trumpet, while others might reflect the contemplative depth of a violin. Recognizing and harnessing these distinct 'musical' traits allows a leader to craft a harmonious ensemble where each member can shine brightest.

Before the first note is played in any musical performance, there's a moment of tuning. Musicians meticulously ensure their instruments harmonize with one another. Drawing a parallel, effective leadership in group settings requires a similar 'tuning' process, which could manifest as team-building exercises, training sessions, or open dialogues. This ensures everyone is aligned in purpose, understanding, and motivation, laying the foundation for a harmonious collective endeavor.

The role of a conductor in an orchestra goes beyond setting the tempo. They breathe life into the score, interpreting its nuances, drawing out emotions, and guiding the orchestra through the narrative of the composition. Likewise, leaders are more than decision-makers; they sense the group's pulse and guide it through the ebbs and flows of dynamics, ensuring each contribution or 'note' finds its rightful place.

Even in the most harmonized settings, moments of discord are inevitable. In music, a note might be missed, a string might snap, or an instrument might falter. Within groups, these disruptions appear as conflicts or misunderstandings. The mark of a skilled leader, much like a seasoned conductor, is in how they navigate these moments. Rather than being derailed, they adapt, reorient, and at times, transform these challenges into unexpected moments of brilliance.

The aftermath of a successful symphony is often punctuated by an encore, an affirmation of resonance with the audience. In the realm of leadership, this encore represents the lasting impact a cohesive group can have, whether it's in the form of achieving unprecedented targets or driving transformative change. It's a reminder that leadership should not only aim to meet expectations but to surpass them, creating legacies that reverberate long after the final note.

The symphony of interactions underscores the delicate yet impactful dance of individual contributions within a collective. It's a vivid testament to the fact that leadership is about celebrating unique strengths while seamlessly integrating them into a resonant, cohesive whole.

Roles and Responsibilities: The Fabric of Group Dynamics

Every group, regardless of its nature or purpose, is a melting pot of diverse individuals, each bringing to the table a unique set of qualities, perspectives, and experiences. These intrinsic attributes often steer individuals towards assuming specific roles within the group, much like players in a theatrical performance.

Imagine a team as a theater stage. Some individuals naturally take center stage, drawing the spotlight with their charisma, confidence, and ability to articulate ideas. These are the vocal proponents, often the face of the group, who articulate its objectives, values, and concerns. Their energy can invigorate discussions and shape the trajectory of group deliberations.

Then, in the shadows, are the silent strategists. These individuals might not always command the stage with grand speeches, but their analytical abilities, deep insights, and thoughtful contributions form the backbone of the group's strategies. They thrive in the details, meticulously charting out plans, foreseeing challenges, and suggesting alternatives. Their strength lies not in the volume of their voice but the depth of their thought.

Adding another layer of complexity are the devil's advocates. These individuals challenge the status quo, question popular opinions, and introduce alternative viewpoints. While they might sometimes be perceived as contrarian, their role is vital. By ensuring that every idea is thoroughly examined and vetted, they safeguard the group against potential oversights and biases.

But the tapestry of roles doesn't end here. There are also the peacemakers who bridge divides and mediate conflicts, the motivators who uplift the group's morale during challenging times, and the implementers who roll up their sleeves and turn strategies into tangible actions.

For a leader, understanding these roles is not just a passive observation but an active responsibility. Leaders must be adept at recognizing the strengths and inclinations of their team members. This involves actively listening, observing, and, at times, even encouraging members to step out of their comfort zones. Once these roles are identified, leaders have the task of positioning each member in a way that maximizes their potential. This could mean giving the silent strategist a platform to present their ideas or pairing the vocal proponent with a devil's advocate to ensure a well-rounded discussion.

The beauty of roles and responsibilities within a group lies in their fluidity. Over time, as group dynamics evolve and individual members grow, these roles might shift and transform. The once silent strategist might find their voice, while the vocal proponent might discover the virtues of listening.

In the grand scheme of group dynamics, ensuring that every member finds their role and purpose is paramount. It's this intricate interplay of roles that paves the way for collaboration, innovation, and the collective realization of goals. For a leader, it's a journey of discovery, alignment, and orchestration, creating a symphony of contributions that drive the group forward.

Conflict and Consensus: Navigating the Dual Edges of Group Dynamics

At the heart of every vibrant group lies a spectrum of opinions, ideas, and perspectives. This diversity, while being the wellspring of innovation, also becomes the fertile ground for conflict. In the multifaceted realm of group dynamics, conflict isn't merely a challenge to be tackled but a catalyst that, when handled with finesse, can propel the group to new heights of understanding and collaboration.

Conflict, in many ways, is the raw, unfiltered voice of diverse viewpoints yearning to be heard. It emerges when deeply held beliefs, values, or approaches clash, and the stakes feel high. For many leaders, the initial response might be to quell the discord or push for a quick resolution. However, this often only provides a temporary reprieve and might suppress underlying issues that could resurface later with greater intensity.

Rather than viewing conflict as a disruptive force, astute leaders recognize it as a mirror reflecting the depth and diversity of their team's collective thought. By approaching conflict with curiosity rather than apprehension, leaders can uncover the root causes, be it a misalignment of goals, a gap in understanding, or a difference in values.

Facilitating open communication is the cornerstone of navigating conflicts. This involves creating a safe space where every member feels empowered to voice their concerns, fears, and suggestions without fear of retribution. Active listening, empathy, and validation are crucial tools in a leader's arsenal during such discussions. It's not about determining who's right or wrong but about understanding the myriad perspectives that make up the tapestry of the group.

Seeking common ground becomes the next phase in the conflict resolution process. Often, beneath the layers of disagreements, there's a shared objective or value that can serve as a unifying force. By highlighting and building upon this shared foundation, leaders can begin the journey from discord to consensus.

It's essential to note that consensus doesn't necessarily mean uniformity. It represents a collective agreement that respects and integrates diverse viewpoints. A well-forged consensus is like a mosaic—each piece retains its individuality, yet together they form a coherent and beautiful picture.

The journey from conflict to consensus often paves the way for innovation. When diverse perspectives collide, they challenge the status quo, prompting the group to think outside the box, explore uncharted territories, and devise novel solutions.

The interplay of conflict and consensus is a testament to the rich tapestry of human interactions within a group. Leaders who harness this dynamic not only ensure the smooth functioning of their teams but also unlock the boundless potential that lies at the intersection of diverse minds. Through the careful navigation of these turbulent yet transformative waters, leaders can craft a group narrative that resonates with harmony, understanding, and shared purpose.

Groupthink and its Pitfalls: The Silent Threat to Collective Wisdom

In the vast spectrum of group dynamics, there lies a seemingly benign, yet insidious phenomenon known as groupthink. On the surface, groupthink may appear as a testament to the group's unity, a reflection of shared perspectives and aligned values. However, beneath this façade of consensus lurks a danger that can undermine the very essence of collaborative decision-making.

Groupthink arises in environments where the quest for unanimity becomes so dominant that it stifles individual creativity, critical thinking, and the expression of alternate viewpoints. The group, in its pursuit of harmony, inadvertently compromises its ability to critically evaluate decisions, leading to choices that may be suboptimal or even detrimental.

Several factors can set the stage for groupthink:

☐ Isolation from External Feedback: Groups that operate in silos, shielded from external opinions and critiques, are more susceptible. Without diverse inputs and the fresh air of external perspectives, the group can become an echo chamber, amplifying shared beliefs and muting dissent.

☐ Directive Leadership: When a leader strongly advocates for a particular decision or viewpoint, it might inadvertently suppress alternative perspectives. Team members might feel pressured to conform, fearing repercussions or wanting to please the leader.

☐ Homogeneity of Group Members: If a group comprises individuals with similar backgrounds, experiences, and ideologies, it reduces the likelihood of diverse perspectives. While such homogeneity can expedite decision-making, it also increases vulnerability to groupthink.

The pitfalls of groupthink are multifaceted. Decisions made under its influence often lack depth and foresight. With no one challenging the status quo or playing devil's advocate, potential flaws or oversights go unexamined. Moreover, when the group's decisions face real-world challenges, the lack of critical evaluation in the decision-making process can lead to unforeseen complications.

For leaders, guarding against groupthink is both a challenge and a responsibility. Here are some strategies to counteract its insidious pull:

☐ Encourage Dissent: Leaders must cultivate an environment where differing opinions are valued. This could involve playing devil's advocate themselves or designating someone to challenge prevailing opinions during discussions.

☐ Seek External Feedback: By bringing in outside experts or perspectives, leaders can introduce fresh viewpoints and disrupt the echo chamber.

☐ Foster Open Communication: Team members should feel safe expressing their thoughts, even if they diverge from the majority. This requires building a culture of trust and respect.

☐ Diversify the Group: A mix of backgrounds, experiences, and perspectives can be the best defense against groupthink. Diversity introduces a natural array of viewpoints, challenging monolithic thinking.

While cohesion and consensus have their merits, the silent specter of groupthink reminds us of the importance of critical thinking and individual voice within collective decision-making. Effective leaders remain vigilant, ensuring that the harmony of group consensus is rooted in deep reflection, robust debate, and a genuine appreciation of diverse perspectives.

The Ripple Effect of Group Dynamics: Echoes Beyond the Immediate Circle

Much like a stone thrown into a pond, the patterns and rhythms of a group have a cascading effect, influencing wider circles of people and systems. This pervasive influence is largely driven by the powerful interplay of shared experiences and collective narratives. When a group embraces a specific ethos — such as a commitment to innovation or a passion for inclusivity — this sentiment often permeates its broader environment. It becomes a vibrant pulse that resonates with others, setting a tone and direction for a wider audience.

Take, for example, a business team fostering a culture of continuous learning and experimentation. Even if this ethos originates within one team, its influence often spills over. Other departments or teams, observing the vibrancy and success of this innovative spirit, might feel inspired to adopt similar practices. Over time, a localized initiative could evolve into a culture shift spanning the entire organization.

In community settings, the initiatives and beliefs of one group can light the way for many. A neighborhood collective emphasizing eco-friendly practices doesn't just impact their immediate surroundings; it can also inspire adjacent communities to embark on their own sustainability journeys. Their initiatives can lead to broader discussions, inspire new local policies, or even motivate businesses to adopt sustainable practices.

For leaders, understanding this ripple effect underscores a profound responsibility and a unique opportunity. By shaping the dynamics of their group, leaders have the ability to prototype new ideas, setting the stage for what can be achieved. Their actions and decisions within the group often set precedents for larger entities, whether it's an entire company or a community. Moreover, the stories and successes that emerge from one group can weave into a broader discourse, influencing narratives and inspiring similar initiatives elsewhere.

The realm of group dynamics, therefore, is not just a microcosm of individual interactions but also a reflection of wider organizational, community, or societal dynamics. Astute leaders recognize this interconnectedness. They understand that their actions and guidance within a group have the potential to reverberate, influencing and inspiring on a much larger scale. Through intentionality and vision, they can harness the power of these ripples, leaving lasting imprints on broader landscapes.

Navigating group dynamics is both an art and a science, demanding a delicate balance of assertiveness and empathy, direction, and flexibility. As we delve deeper into the intricate web of human interactions, we'll uncover strategies and insights to help aspiring leaders foster groups that are not just functional but truly transformative. Leadership, after all, is as much about guiding individuals as it is about shaping and being shaped by the collective journey.

Power and Influence: The Invisible Threads of Leadership

Few threads are as impactful, yet as elusive, as power and influence. While both elements play a foundational role in the realm of leadership, their manifestations can be diverse, subtle, and often intertwined. To truly grasp the essence of leadership and to navigate its complex terrain, it's imperative to delve into the nuances of these two forces.

Power is often perceived as the capacity to direct or influence the behavior of others or the course of events. It can emanate from various sources: a formal position, expertise in a field, control over resources, or even personal charisma. Yet, power is not just about possessing authority; it's about how that authority is wielded. Leadership is not synonymous with mere power possession but is intricately linked to its judicious application. The best leaders understand that power is a responsibility, not just a privilege.

Influence, on the other hand, delves deeper into the realm of the intangible. It's the ability to shape perspectives, inspire actions, and mold outcomes, often without explicit authority. While power can be conferred, influence is typically earned. It's built on trust, credibility, and genuine connections. Influence thrives on the leader's ability to resonate with others, to understand their motivations, and to align them with a shared vision or goal.

The dance between power and influence is intricate. While they can exist independently, their convergence can create leadership magic. A leader with power but devoid of influence might find compliance but not commitment. Conversely, a leader rich in influence but lacking in formal power can inspire but might struggle to effect tangible change without the necessary authority or resources.

The duality of power and influence brings forth several key reflections for aspiring and established leaders alike:

☐ Understanding Power Sources: Recognizing where one's power originates from can help leaders use it more effectively. Is it derived from a formal title, expertise, or perhaps personal charisma?

☐ Cultivating Influence: Building genuine relationships, showcasing expertise, and demonstrating consistency are pathways to earning influence. How can leaders foster trust and credibility?

☐ Balancing Power and Influence: How can leaders ensure they're not over-relying on one at the expense of the other? When is it time to flex power, and when is it more prudent to lean on influence?

☐ Ethical Considerations: With great power comes great responsibility. Leaders must reflect on the ethical implications of their actions and decisions, ensuring they wield their power and influence with integrity.

Navigating the realms of power and influence requires astute awareness and finesse. Their subtleties often lie below the surface, yet their impacts can resonate deeply in the landscape of leadership.

Within the core of power, there are multifaceted dimensions. Beyond the traditional hierarchical power, which is often associated with positions and titles, several nuanced forms of power shape the dynamics of leadership. One of these is expert power, stemming from knowledge, skills, or expertise in a particular area. This type of power sees leaders being recognized and sought after for their specialized guidance and advice.

Referent power is another, grounded in interpersonal relationships, with leaders admired and respected for their charisma, integrity, or other personal traits. On the other hand, reward power is rooted in a leader's ability to distribute rewards such as bonuses, promotions, and praise, motivating through positive reinforcement. Contrastingly, coercive power is centered on the potential to mete out punishments or remove privileges, which can lead to compliance but may also breed resentment if overused. Finally, in today's data-driven world, informational power, derived from possessing valuable knowledge or information, holds significant sway.

Complementing the dimensions of power are various influence tactics that leaders can employ. Effective leaders skillfully deploy these tactics based on the situation at hand. Persuasion, for instance, involves articulating points both logically and emotionally to sway opinions. Inspiration can stir emotions and passion by painting a vivid picture of a vision or cause. Consultation takes a more collaborative approach, engaging others in the decision-making process and valuing their expertise. Working alongside others and pooling resources is the essence of collaboration, while negotiation focuses on seeking a win-win situation through mutual understanding and compromise.

It's essential to note that power and influence are not static constructs. They're dynamic entities that evolve based on a leader's actions, decisions, and the shifting environment they operate within. As such, leaders must be agile, continuously recalibrating their approach to ensure they remain relevant, respected, and effective.

As leaders traverse the corridors of power and influence, the ethical aspect cannot be sidestepped. These forces are potent tools for leadership but come with substantial responsibilities. Misusing power can lead to manipulation or exploitation, and misdirected influence can result in misinformation or undue pressure. Thus, the essence of leadership lies not just in harnessing these forces but in wielding them with a strong moral compass. Continuous reflection upon intentions and actions is paramount to ensure leaders act in the best interests of those they serve.

Conformity, Compliance, and Obedience: Navigating the Social Forces in Leadership

In the realm of social interactions and leadership, understanding how individuals align their behaviors with group norms or authoritative demands is vital. Conformity, compliance, and obedience are foundational concepts in this domain, each offering a unique perspective on the dynamics of group behavior and individual choices within broader societal or organizational contexts.

Conformity delves into the subtle pressures individuals feel to fit in or adhere to societal norms and group expectations. It's the unspoken force that prompts us to align our beliefs, attitudes, and actions with those of the majority, often without any explicit prompts. While conformity can foster unity and harmonious interactions, it also carries the risk of stifling individuality and suppressing dissenting voices. For leaders, the challenge lies in fostering a culture where team members feel the freedom to express diverse viewpoints while still working collaboratively towards a shared goal.

Compliance, on the other hand, speaks to the act of willingly changing one's behavior in response to a direct request, often from someone without any formal authority over the individual. While compliance might seem superficial, it provides insights into how people can be persuaded or motivated to align with a certain direction or decision, even if temporarily. Leaders can leverage the principles of compliance to encourage desired behaviors, but they must be cautious to ensure that the requests are ethical, fair, and for the collective good.

Diving deeper into the power dynamics, Obedience examines the extent to which individuals follow orders or directives from those in authority. Rooted deeply in hierarchical structures and power relations, obedience can be a double-edged sword. While it can facilitate order and discipline, excessive obedience can also lead to unquestioning allegiance and potentially harmful actions, especially if the authority figure's directives are misguided.

The interplay between conformity, compliance, and obedience paints a vivid picture of the intricate dance between individual agency and collective pressures in both societal and organizational settings. Leaders stand at the crossroads of these forces, tasked with the responsibility to guide, inspire, and sometimes challenge their teams. They must strike a delicate balance—ensuring alignment and cohesion without stifling the rich tapestry of diverse thoughts, experiences, and aspirations that each team member brings to the table.

Conformity is the silent nudge that influences us to mirror the beliefs, attitudes, or behaviors of the majority. It stems from an inherent desire for acceptance and the fear of being ostracized. Leaders often encounter the effects of conformity when team members hesitate to voice divergent opinions, preferring to go with the flow. While conformity can lead to cohesion and a harmonious work environment, it also poses challenges. There's the danger of perpetuating a status quo, which may hinder innovation, or suppressing the rich diversity of thought that often drives progress. As leaders, fostering an environment where individuals can balance the desire to fit in with the courage to stand out becomes paramount.

Differing from the subtle forces of conformity, **compliance** emerges when individuals adjust their behavior based on a direct request, often without considering the authority or position of the person making the request. The realm of compliance offers valuable insights into persuasion and the dynamics of assent. Leaders, when making requests or proposing directions, tap into the underpinnings of compliance. It underscores the significance of clear communication, the value of reasoning, and the art of persuasion in leadership. However, the ethical dimension is crucial. Using compliance strategies requires ensuring they are employed for collective benefit, grounded in fairness and respect.

Obedience delves deeper, anchored in the relationship between authority and subordinates. It's the act of following orders or directives from those perceived as authority figures. In structured environments, like organizations, obedience can be essential for maintaining order and discipline. However, it's not without its perils. Blind obedience, where directives are followed without question, can lead to harmful actions or decisions, especially if the authority's commands are flawed or unethical. Leaders, therefore, bear the responsibility of exercising their authority judiciously, encouraging constructive questioning, and ensuring that the path they chart is ethical and inclusive.

To appreciate the vast scope of leadership is to recognize its interplay with these elemental forces of social behavior. Every leader, regardless of the context or domain, will invariably encounter the dynamics of conformity, compliance, and obedience. They serve as reminders that leadership is not a one-way avenue of command but a complex journey through shared human experiences.

It is vital for leaders to remain attuned to these dynamics, not just as abstract concepts but as real, tangible forces that shape decisions, actions, and interactions within groups. They must be discerning enough to embrace the strengths these behaviors offer while staying vigilant against their potential pitfalls.

In the broader spectrum of leadership, these dynamics underscore the importance of ethical grounding, open communication, and mutual respect. Leaders must cultivate environments where individuals feel empowered to think critically, question constructively, and contribute authentically.

As we transition to other facets of social psychology and leadership in subsequent sections, it's essential to carry forward these insights. They form the foundational understanding upon which more complex leadership strategies and nuances are built.

In essence, a nuanced grasp of conformity, compliance, and obedience offers leaders a roadmap to navigate the vast and intricate landscape of human behavior, ensuring that their leadership journey is both impactful and empathetic.

Exercise 4: Exploring Conformity, Compliance, and Obedience in Your Leadership Journey

Objective: To deepen your understanding of the subtle differences between conformity, compliance, and obedience, and to recognize their real-world implications in leadership.

Craft Your Scenario: Form small groups with your classmates, ideally 4-5 students per group. Within your group, collaboratively create a brief role-play scenario that illustrates either conformity, compliance, or obedience in a leadership context. Aim for clarity, ensuring your scenario distinctly represents only one of these concepts.

Showcase Your Understanding:
It's performance time! Each group will present their role-play to the rest of the class. After you've watched a performance, identify which concept (conformity, compliance, or obedience) you believe was portrayed and be ready to share your reasoning.

Engage in Collective Reflection:
☐ Once all groups have performed, let's engage in a collective discussion. Consider these guiding questions:
☐ Were there any scenarios that particularly struck a chord with you? Why?
☐ In which scenarios did you feel the leader's actions were ethically questionable?

- As future leaders, how do you think you can promote constructive feedback while minimizing unhelpful conformity, compliance, or obedience?
- Think about your own experiences. Can you recall instances where you've felt the tug of these dynamics? How did they play out?

Introspection Time:
- Take a moment to jot down your personal reflections:
- Recall a moment when you might have conformed, complied, or obeyed, even if you weren't entirely in agreement.
- Ponder over how you felt during that instance and any outcomes that followed, whether they were positive or negative.
- With the benefit of hindsight and today's discussion, how might you approach similar situations differently, especially if you're in a leadership role?

Wrapping Up:
Leadership is as much about self-awareness as it is about guiding others. By understanding our natural inclinations, whether it's to conform, comply, or obey, we're better equipped to lead with intention, fostering environments where everyone feels valued and heard. Remember, your leadership journey is ongoing, and every experience, reflection, and lesson, like today's, will shape the leader you're becoming. Embrace the journey and continue to grow!

Chapter 5: Gender, Diversity, and Leadership

Individual threads of gender, culture, and diversity interweave to form intricate patterns that demand our attention and understanding. This chapter delves into the heart of one of the most transformative shifts in leadership dynamics: the recognition and celebration of the rich mosaic of gender and diversity, and the roles they play in shaping modern leadership paradigms.

Historically, leadership narratives have often been monochromatic, dominated by a singular perspective, usually male and rooted in specific cultural contexts. But as the world evolved, societies changed, and boundaries blurred, there emerged a pressing need to broaden our understanding of leadership to include voices and visions previously marginalized or overlooked. This expansion of perspective does not merely cater to a social or moral imperative; it reflects a practical understanding that diverse leadership is robust leadership, resilient in the face of challenges and adaptive in the face of change.

Take, for instance, the rising prominence of women in leadership roles. Their journey, fraught with challenges, battles against stereotypes, and the weight of historical biases, offers a testament to resilience, adaptability, and the ability to lead with empathy and strength. The narratives of women leaders provide invaluable lessons about balancing power with grace, authority with care, and ambition with compassion.

But our discourse on diversity in leadership is not complete without recognizing the kaleidoscope of cultural contexts. Cultural norms, values, and expectations shape leadership styles, decision-making processes, and interpersonal dynamics. As our world grows increasingly interconnected, leaders find themselves at the crossroads of various cultural influences, navigating differences, and finding common grounds.

In a globalized era, leading in a diverse world has become an imperative rather than a choice. With teams spread across geographies, clientele spanning continents, and stakeholders from varied backgrounds, leaders are called upon to be cultural translators, diversity champions, and inclusive visionaries.

Women in Leadership Roles

Over the decades, women have carved out significant spaces for themselves in the professional world, shattering glass ceilings and defying societal expectations. Their journey to leadership positions, however, hasn't been without its challenges. Despite progress, the landscape of leadership still bears imprints of historical biases and entrenched stereotypes, presenting unique challenges and experiences for women.

Historically, leadership was often viewed through a predominantly masculine lens, favoring attributes traditionally associated with men such as decisiveness, assertiveness, and control. Women, meanwhile, were often typecast into roles that emphasized empathy, nurturing, and cooperation. While these traits are invaluable in leadership, the narrow definitions and societal confines limited women's perceived capabilities in top-tier positions.

The tides began to change in the latter half of the 20th century as women started making notable strides in various fields. From politics to business, academia to activism, women began to claim positions of influence and authority. This rise was not merely numerical but also brought about a paradigm shift in the understanding of leadership itself. Women leaders introduced and emphasized a more collaborative, inclusive, and empathetic leadership style, validating that these traditionally "feminine" attributes held immense power in fostering innovation, team cohesion, and organizational growth.

Despite these strides, women leaders often find themselves walking a tightrope. They grapple with the 'double bind' dilemma - being authoritative without being labeled aggressive or being empathetic without being seen as weak. The societal microscope under which women leaders operate often magnifies their mistakes while overshadowing their accomplishments.

The narratives of women in leadership roles are overwhelmingly those of resilience and reinvention. They adapt, persist, and often bring transformative changes to their organizations. Take, for instance, the increase in organizational policies emphasizing work-life balance, well-being, and mental health – areas where women leaders have often been pioneers.

The influence of women in top leadership roles is not merely anecdotal; it is backed by rigorous research and tangible results. The presence of women in these positions seems to correlate with enhanced organizational performance on multiple fronts, showcasing the profound impact of gender diversity on corporate health.

Research has consistently indicated that organizations with women in top leadership roles often outperform their counterparts in various metrics, from profitability to innovation. Their unique perspectives, lived experiences, and leadership styles offer a blend of strategic acumen, emotional intelligence, and holistic vision.

One notable area of influence is profitability. Multiple studies have shown that companies with women in C-suite positions or on their boards tend to have higher profit margins than those without. This could be attributed to the diverse decision-making processes and strategies women bring to the table, which often focus on long-term sustainability and holistic growth. Diversity, in any form, allows for a variety of perspectives, leading to comprehensive problem-solving and more innovative strategies.

Beyond profitability, innovation thrives in environments where diverse viewpoints are welcomed. Women leaders, with their unique lived experiences and perspectives, often challenge the status quo and introduce fresh approaches to traditional problems. By doing so, they foster a culture of continuous learning and adaptation. When employees see leadership that is unafraid to think outside the box, they too feel encouraged to push boundaries and venture into uncharted territories.

Women's leadership styles often stand out in their emphasis on collaboration, inclusivity, and emotional intelligence. This fosters an organizational culture where team members feel valued and heard, leading to higher job satisfaction and reduced turnover. By tapping into emotional intelligence, women leaders can more effectively navigate interpersonal dynamics, build strong teams, and create a harmonious work environment.

Their holistic vision often ensures that decisions aren't made in silos but are seen in the larger context of organizational well-being. Whether it's employee welfare, environmental considerations, or societal impact, women leaders often weigh the broader implications of business decisions. This not only ensures sustainability but also bolsters the organization's reputation in the eyes of stakeholders, consumers, and potential employees.

The fabric of an organization isn't just made up of its financial assets or its products; it's intricately woven with its values, ethos, strategies, and most importantly, its people. The inclusion of women in leadership roles introduces new threads to this fabric, making it richer and more diverse. With these new threads come fresh perspectives and approaches, which can fundamentally change the way an organization functions.

Historically, many businesses and institutions have operated within a largely homogenous framework, often characterized by a top-down, singular approach to decision-making. Such a system, though efficient in some respects, can limit an organization's adaptability, creativity, and capacity for genuine growth. Women in leadership positions disrupt this status quo. They bring a range of experiences, insights, and managerial styles that promote inclusivity and collaboration, which are vital in today's rapidly changing business landscape.

A more inclusive approach means that decisions are made with a broader set of stakeholders in mind. This adaptability ensures that organizations can pivot more readily in the face of challenges, whether they are market downturns, technological disruptions, or societal changes. An adaptive organization is more resilient, agile, and attuned to the nuances of its environment.

The consistent success of organizations led by women isn't just a testament to their capability but is also reflective of the benefits of diversity. Such organizations are often more innovative, as diversity fosters a culture where multiple viewpoints collide, leading to breakthrough ideas. They are also more attuned to their stakeholders, as a diverse leadership team can better understand and cater to a diverse customer base.

This outperformance isn't merely a statistical anomaly but a compelling narrative that drives home the importance of diversifying leadership. It's a narrative that champions the breaking of glass ceilings and the dismantling of barriers that have historically kept women from these roles. When we see the tangible benefits that women leaders bring, the argument for greater representation becomes not just about equity but also about business excellence.

So, when we say that the presence of women in leadership roles transforms organizations, it isn't mere rhetoric. It's a reflection of a deeper shift – a move from traditional, unilateral decision-making structures to dynamic, multifaceted, and inclusive ones. It's a celebration of the fact that when diverse voices are at the helm, organizations don't just succeed in the conventional sense; they thrive in ways previously unimagined.

Cultural Aspects of Leadership

Culture profoundly influences how people perceive leadership, and this influence extends across both national and organizational lines. At the heart of culture lie values, beliefs, and norms that shape how individuals think, behave, and interact with one another. Leadership, being a relational activity, is thus deeply embedded in and shaped by these cultural frameworks.

Across different cultures, the expectations and definitions of a "good" leader vary. For instance, while Western cultures, particularly those in North America and Europe, often emphasize individualism, autonomy, and direct communication, many Eastern cultures stress the importance of collectivism, harmony, and indirect communication. These fundamental differences can lead to varied leadership styles. In the West, a transformational and participative style, where leaders inspire and involve their teams in decision-making processes, might be preferred. In contrast, in many Eastern cultures, there's a greater emphasis on hierarchy and respect for authority, leading to a more directive style of leadership.

Cultural intelligence has become an invaluable skill for leaders in our increasingly globalized world. Leaders with high cultural intelligence can effectively navigate, work, and lead in cross-cultural settings. They understand that leadership isn't a one-size-fits-all concept but is, in fact, malleable, shaped by the cultural nuances of the environment they are in.

Apart from national cultures, organizational cultures also play a significant role in leadership dynamics. Every organization, irrespective of its size, has a unique culture that defines its values, working style, and approach to challenges. Leaders within an organization play a pivotal role in both shaping and being shaped by this culture. For instance, a start-up might have a culture that values agility, innovation, and risk-taking, while a century-old conglomerate might prioritize stability, processes, and tradition. Leadership styles would, naturally, differ in these two environments.

In today's interconnected world, the challenges and intricacies of leading across cultural boundaries have become an inevitable part of a leader's journey. As businesses expand, forge new alliances, or enter untapped markets, leaders often grapple with the complexities that arise from these intercultural intersections. The dynamics of global teams, for example, require a refined skill set that goes beyond traditional leadership capabilities. The layers of cultural nuance, differing communication styles, and varying workplace norms add layers of complexity to leadership roles.

When leaders find themselves at the helm of a diverse team spread across continents, they are presented with an unparalleled opportunity and challenge. On one hand, they have a tapestry of insights, experiences, and perspectives that can lead to innovative solutions and creative problem-solving. On the other, they must navigate the potential pitfalls of misunderstandings, differing work ethics, and contrasting values. In such settings, it becomes imperative for leaders to foster an environment of mutual respect, open communication, and shared purpose.

Mergers and acquisitions offer another dimension where the confluence of distinct corporate cultures is evident. When two firms, each with its own set of values, beliefs, and practices, come together, the process is not just about integrating systems and processes but also about melding two often very different organizational cultures. Leaders play a pivotal role in steering such mergers towards success. They must appreciate the strengths of both cultures, address concerns, bridge gaps, and craft a cohesive, harmonized culture that members from both former entities can identify with and feel a part of.

A key aspect of navigating these multicultural challenges is the concept of cultural intelligence. It's the ability to recognize, understand, and respect cultural differences and to adapt one's leadership style accordingly. It's about being aware of one's own cultural biases and being open to learning and adapting. In essence, it's a blend of empathy, adaptability, and knowledge.

Leaders who actively invest in developing their cultural intelligence are better poised to harness the potential of diverse teams, successfully navigate mergers, and build organizations that are truly global in thought and action. As the business landscape continues to evolve, the ability to lead with a global mindset, appreciating and leveraging cultural nuances, will be among the most sought-after leadership qualities.

Leading in a diverse world presents both unique challenges and unparalleled opportunities. As globalization brings people from various backgrounds, ethnicities, religions, and orientations into closer contact, it becomes essential for leaders to cultivate an inclusive mindset. Such a mindset not only embraces diversity but also views it as a fundamental strength of any organization.

The term 'diversity' often conjures images of demographic differences such as race, gender, and age. However, in the broader context of leadership, it encompasses a vast range of individual attributes and experiences, including educational backgrounds, socio-economic statuses, cognitive styles, skill sets, and even life experiences. As leaders contend with this multifaceted web of individual differences, the task becomes about more than just recognizing or tolerating diversity; it's about leveraging these differences for organizational success.

In a diverse world, leaders are increasingly tasked with building bridges. They must facilitate cross-cultural understanding and ensure that all voices, regardless of their origin or nature, are heard and valued. This requires an acute awareness of unconscious biases that might influence decisions, as well as a proactive effort to minimize their effects. Leaders must also actively foster environments where diverse teams can thrive, promoting collaboration and mutual respect.

Leadership in a diverse world means understanding the varied needs and aspirations of a heterogeneous client base. As markets become increasingly global, products and services must cater to a wide range of cultural tastes, preferences, and values. Leaders who can anticipate these needs, tap into local insights, and tailor their offerings accordingly will be at a distinct advantage.

The benefits of leading in a diverse world extend beyond just organizational performance metrics. Diverse teams often bring a richer array of solutions to problems, foster creativity, and promote innovation. They provide different perspectives that can challenge the status quo and inspire novel approaches. Additionally, organizations that champion diversity and inclusion are often viewed more favorably, helping attract top talent and even influencing consumer choices.

The rapid pace of globalization has transformed the way businesses operate, introducing a spectrum of complexities and opportunities. In this era of interconnectedness and interdependence, leadership requires a keen understanding of diverse cultures, traditions, and perspectives to make informed decisions. Leaders are no longer confined to the local or national scene but must consider the global implications of their choices.

☐ The Necessity of Adaptation: Gone are the days when leaders could operate within a familiar set of cultural norms. As business operations expand beyond borders, so too must the horizons of those at the helm. Adapting isn't just about understanding foreign markets or global economic trends; it's about appreciating the subtle nuances that influence human behavior, motivation, and values in different parts of the world. Such understanding is paramount to effectively lead teams, negotiate with partners, and resonate with customers worldwide.

☐ Honing Skills for the Global Arena: Today's leaders need a set of skills tailored to the global arena. Cultural intelligence, for instance, becomes invaluable. This form of intelligence goes beyond simple cultural awareness, encompassing the ability to adapt behaviors and strategies in response to diverse cultural contexts. Similarly, global leaders must develop a keen sense for geopolitical shifts and their potential business ramifications, a skill that demands a mix of historical knowledge, current affairs insight, and forward-looking acumen.

☐ Expanding Perspectives through Continuous Learning: The most effective leaders are those who commit to lifelong learning. This means not only keeping abreast of industry trends and innovations but also delving into the histories, languages, and philosophies of the various cultures they interact with. Such comprehensive understanding facilitates deeper connections, engenders trust, and allows for more authentic interactions.

☐ Embracing the Rich Tapestry of Diversity: Diversity is not just a buzzword; it's a powerhouse of untapped potential. Varied life experiences, worldviews, and cognitive styles come together to create a mosaic of perspectives. When leveraged correctly, this diversity can lead to innovative solutions, creative problem-solving, and robust strategies that cater to a global audience. Leaders must create environments where differences are celebrated, where every voice is valued, and where the collective wisdom of diverse teams is harnessed for shared success.

☐ Navigating Challenges with Empathy and Inclusivity: As leaders encounter unfamiliar territories, they're bound to face challenges. Some of these challenges may arise from misunderstandings or misinterpretations rooted in cultural differences. In such instances, empathy becomes a leader's most potent tool. By striving to understand others' viewpoints and emotions, leaders can foster mutual respect and bridge divides.

Historically, leadership structures, particularly in the corporate world, were predominantly male-centric, often sidelining women or relegating them to roles with limited decision-making power. This was not just a reflection of workplace bias but echoed broader societal norms that hesitated to see women as decision-makers and visionaries.

As societies progressed and as the corporate landscape underwent shifts, the narrative began to change. Women began breaking glass ceilings, proving time and again that leadership knows no gender. What became increasingly evident was that women leaders often brought unique perspectives, combining strength with empathy, assertiveness with understanding, and vision with inclusivity.

Their ascent to leadership roles has often been marked by challenges. Bias, both overt and subconscious, hurdles in work-life balance, and lack of representation in certain sectors meant that every step was hard-earned. But with every challenge surmounted, they set a precedent, forging a path for future generations.

Organizations helmed by women often see increased profitability, more innovation, and a holistic approach to problem-solving. Such empirical evidence dispels any remaining myths about the capabilities of women leaders. The leadership qualities they exhibit—whether it's resilience in the face of adversity, emotional intelligence that fosters team unity, or strategic acumen shaped by multifaceted life experiences—underscore the importance of having diverse voices at the decision-making table.

Women leaders often act as role models, not just for aspiring women leaders, but for anyone who believes in the principles of equity, resilience, and meritocracy. Their stories inspire, their visions guide, and their journeys underscore the essence of modern leadership.

Diversity, in all its forms, enriches leadership. Just as a blend of different cultures and backgrounds offers varied perspectives, so does a balance of genders. When we look at leadership through the lens of gender, it's not just about representation. It's about reshaping the very paradigms of leadership, infusing it with varied experiences, insights, and visions.

To truly harness the potential of our diverse, interconnected world, we must champion leaders from all backgrounds, regardless of gender or other differentiating factors. Only by doing so can organizations, societies, and nations thrive in an era marked by rapid change and global interdependence.

Exercise 5: Navigating Leadership Diversity - Role Reversal Simulation

Objective: To understand and appreciate the various challenges, perspectives, and advantages that come with diverse leadership. As part of our exploration into diversity in leadership, we're going to undertake a hands-on exercise designed to provide insights into different leadership perspectives and challenges. The purpose of this simulation is to put you in the shoes of someone quite different from yourself, helping you gain an empathetic understanding of diverse leadership experiences.

Instructions:

Formation of Groups:
- Please divide yourselves into small groups of 5.
- Each group will be assigned various leadership scenarios rooted in real-world challenges faced by diverse leaders.

Scenario Assignment: Each group will receive a packet detailing a specific leadership scenario. This scenario might describe challenges faced by a female CEO in a male-dominated industry, a young leader managing a team of older employees, or a foreign executive navigating leadership in a different cultural context.

Role Reversal:
- Within each group, one student will assume the role of the leader described in the scenario. The remaining members will act as team members, stakeholders, or board members.
- Those in leadership roles must respond to challenges and tasks described in the scenario, while the others will react, question, or support as per the given instructions.

Discussion and Reflection: After navigating through the scenarios, each group will discuss their experiences. Reflect on the challenges faced, how the leader's diverse background influenced decisions, and the advantages that diversity brought to the table. One member from each group will then share their group's reflections with the entire class.

Class-wide Debrief: We will reconvene as a class and discuss the overarching themes, challenges, and learnings that emerged from the simulation. We will also explore potential strategies and solutions for the challenges faced in each scenario.

Through this exercise, you will: Gain firsthand experience of the challenges diverse leaders might face. Understand the advantages and unique perspectives diverse leaders can bring to an organization. Develop empathetic leadership skills by stepping into the shoes of someone with a different background or experience. Enhance your collaborative and adaptive problem-solving skills. Remember, diversity in leadership isn't just a "nice-to-have" – it's a crucial component of modern, effective, and resilient leadership. Through exercises like this, we aim to equip you with the understanding and skills necessary to navigate and champion diversity in your future leadership roles.

Chapter 6: Organizational Behavior (OB)

At the heart of every successful organization lies a complex tapestry of human behaviors, interactions, and relationships. While the products, services, or technologies offered by an organization are essential, it's the human element—the dynamic interplay of individual personalities, team dynamics, and overarching organizational culture—that often dictates an organization's success or failure. This is the realm of organizational behavior, a field that delves into the intricacies of human behavior within the context of organizations.

In today's rapidly evolving business landscape, understanding organizational behavior has never been more crucial. As businesses grapple with challenges like globalization, technological advancements, and shifting demographics, the importance of optimizing the human side of operations becomes evident. It's not just about having a strategy or the right resources; it's about understanding how individuals think, how teams operate, and how an organization's culture can either drive innovation or stifle it.

This chapter, "Organizational Behavior," aims to illuminate the depths of human behavior within the workplace. We'll explore the myriad factors that influence an individual's attitudes, perceptions, and motivations. We'll delve into team dynamics, shedding light on the processes that foster collaboration and those that lead to conflict. Leadership, an essential aspect of organizational behavior, will be examined, revealing how leaders can shape and influence the culture and climate of their organizations. Moreover, as we navigate through the chapter, we'll constantly emphasize the importance of communication, decision-making, and change management, key pillars that support the infrastructure of a well-functioning organization.

The study of organizational behavior is not just about understanding how organizations work. It's about equipping business leaders, managers, and employees with insights and tools to create more effective, harmonious, and successful workplaces. In this chapter, we invite you to delve into this fascinating world, where psychology meets business, and where human potential meets organizational success.

In the realm of business and management, there exists a specialized area that delves into the core of what makes organizations tick: Organizational Behavior (OB). But what is it exactly, and why is it so vital in today's complex corporate ecosystem?

Definition and Importance of Studying Organizational Behavior

Organizational Behavior, at its essence, is the comprehensive study of human behavior within organizations. It's an interdisciplinary field that merges insights from psychology, sociology, anthropology, and economics to understand the intricate dance of human actions, interactions, and reactions in a workplace setting. OB doesn't just focus on the behaviors themselves but seeks to uncover the underlying motivations, perceptions, emotions, and values that drive those behaviors.

Understanding organizational behavior is crucial for multiple reasons. First and foremost, organizations are made up of people. The efficiency, productivity, and overall health of any organization are directly tied to the well-being, motivation, and behaviors of its members. By studying OB, leaders and managers can better predict and comprehend the complex human dynamics at play, leading to more informed decision-making processes.

As businesses grow and evolve, the challenges they face become multifaceted. With issues ranging from conflict resolution to ensuring effective communication, from managing organizational change to fostering innovation, understanding the nuances of human behavior becomes paramount. For organizations to thrive, they need to be more than just financially or technologically sound; they need to be human-centric, placing people and their behaviors at the core of their operational strategies.

The Interplay Between Individuals, Groups, and the Organization as a Whole

The beauty and complexity of organizational behavior stem from the intricate interplay between different levels: individuals, groups or teams, and the organization at large. Each level, while distinct, deeply influences and is influenced by the others.

At the individual level, factors such as personality, perception, motivation, and job satisfaction play pivotal roles in determining how a person behaves within an organization. These individual behaviors, in turn, influence and are shaped by group dynamics. When individuals come together to form teams or groups, new behavioral patterns emerge. Group norms, roles, and conflicts come into play, shaping the behaviors of the group as a collective entity.

Zooming out further, these groups operate within the broader framework of the organization. The organization's culture, structure, and leadership styles set the tone for both individual and group behaviors. This overarching organizational umbrella determines the policies, procedures, and values that guide how members of the organization interact with one another and with external stakeholders.

The backbone of any organization is its workforce, each member bringing a unique blend of experiences, traits, and perspectives to the table. To truly grasp organizational behavior, it's essential to first understand the foundational elements that dictate individual behavior. While myriad factors influence how a person acts within a workplace, some elements consistently emerge as crucial determinants.

Personality and Work Behavior

Every individual is a mosaic of traits that define their personality. This constellation of traits—ranging from openness to experience to conscientiousness—plays a significant role in shaping an individual's approach to work. For instance, someone high in extraversion might thrive in team-based projects and roles that require frequent interpersonal interactions. In contrast, an individual with a high degree of neuroticism might be more sensitive to workplace stress or criticism.

But it's not just about how personality influences work behavior. The organizational environment also impacts how personality traits are expressed. A rigid, hierarchical company structure might stifle the creativity of someone high in openness, while a flexible, startup environment might amplify it.

Perception and Individual Decision-Making

Every day, individuals in an organization make countless decisions, both minor and critical. Underlying these decisions is the complex process of perception—the way individuals select, organize, and interpret the vast amount of information they encounter. This perceptual process is deeply personal, filtered through each individual's past experiences, biases, and cultural background.

For instance, two managers might perceive the same employee's performance differently based on their individual biases or past interactions with the employee. These perceptions, in turn, influence their decision-making, from feedback they provide to the employee to decisions about promotions or raises.

Attitudes, Job Satisfaction, and Motivation

Attitudes are evaluative statements or judgments concerning objects, people, or events. In the workplace, attitudes can span a range of topics, from feelings about a particular project to opinions about organizational leadership. These attitudes, especially when they relate to job satisfaction, have profound implications for organizational outcomes. A satisfied employee is more likely to be motivated, loyal, and productive.

Motivation, the driving force behind all human actions, is particularly crucial in a work context. While it's partly intrinsic, stemming from an individual's internal desires and goals, it's also heavily influenced by external factors. Organizational rewards, recognition, opportunities for growth, and the nature of the job itself can all bolster or diminish an employee's motivation.

Work Teams and Groups

The modern organizational landscape has increasingly recognized the value of collaboration, with work teams and groups becoming essential units of productivity. Rather than operating as isolated individuals, employees collaborate, brainstorm, and tackle challenges together, harnessing the collective wisdom and varied skills of their team members. This collaborative spirit, however, comes with its own complexities, shaped by the nature of teams, the dynamics within them, and the inevitable conflicts that arise.

Types of Teams

There's no one-size-fits-all when it comes to teams in the workplace. Organizations employ a variety of team structures to address specific needs:

☐ Functional Teams: These teams are organized around specific functions or departments, like marketing, finance, or human resources. Members typically share similar skills and expertise and work on tasks that fall within their function.

☐ Cross-Functional Teams: Comprising members from different departments or functions, these teams are formed to achieve a common goal. They bring together diverse perspectives and expertise, often leading to innovative solutions.

☐ Virtual Teams: The digital age and the rise of remote work have made virtual teams commonplace. These teams consist of members who may be geographically dispersed but collaborate using technology, from video conferencing to collaboration platforms.

Group Dynamics

The internal mechanics of how a team functions—its dynamics—can make or break its success. Several stages typically mark the life of a group: forming (when members first come together), storming (where conflicts and differences emerge), norming (establishing routines and roles), performing (when the team starts to achieve its objectives), and adjourning (when the team's goal is met or the project ends).

Within these stages, certain aspects play pivotal roles:

☐ Norms: Every team develops its own set of unwritten rules or norms that dictate expected behaviors. These might revolve around punctuality, communication etiquette, or even dress codes.

☐ Roles: Over time, members naturally settle into specific roles within the team, whether it's the brainstormer, the critic, the harmonizer, or the executor.

☐ Cohesion: This refers to the strength of the bond between team members. A highly cohesive team typically experiences better collaboration and higher morale.

Managing Conflict within Teams

Conflict, while often perceived negatively, is a natural part of team interactions. When managed effectively, it can lead to deeper understanding, clearer communication, and innovative solutions. However, unchecked or mismanaged conflict can disrupt team harmony and hinder performance.

Leaders and team members must be adept at identifying sources of conflict, whether they stem from differences in opinion, perceived inequities, or clashes in personalities. Effective conflict management strategies, from open communication to third-party mediation, can ensure that disagreements become steppingstones to better collaboration rather than obstacles.

The realm of work teams and groups is intricate, influenced by the type of team, its internal dynamics, and the challenges it faces. By understanding these nuances, organizations can foster a culture of effective teamwork, driving productivity and innovation in tandem.

Leadership in Organizational Behavior

Within the intricate tapestry of an organization, leadership acts as a guiding thread, weaving together various elements to form a cohesive whole. Every individual in an organization plays their part, but it's often the leaders who cast the longest shadow, influencing not just the nuts and bolts of day-to-day operations but also the more intangible aspects of workplace culture, collaboration, and morale.

Distinguishing between leadership and management is a topic that has generated much discourse. Management primarily focuses on tasks: ensuring they are completed, that resources are optimized, and that targets are achieved. It is rooted in the activities of planning, organizing, and supervising. Leadership delves into the deeper realm of human interactions and motivations. Leaders are visionaries who inspire and galvanize their teams towards shared goals. They create environments that foster innovation, ensure that team members feel appreciated and valued, and drive the organization forward by constantly challenging the status quo.

Different leadership styles can drastically alter the organizational atmosphere:

Autocratic Leaders tend to make decisions without much consultation. This can lead to rapid decision-making but may suppress creativity and leave employees feeling sidelined.

On the flip side, **Democratic Leaders** involve their teams in decision processes, boosting morale and ownership feelings, even though it might occasionally slow things down.

Transformational Leaders not only set ambitious goals but also passionately motivate their teams to achieve them, challenging them to surpass their own limits.

In contrast, **Laissez-faire Leaders** allow their teams considerable freedom. While this can lead to innovative outcomes, it risks a lack of guidance or direction.

Each leadership style, with its distinct approach, has a unique impact on aspects like team collaboration, communication channels, innovative capacity, and the overall health of the organization. Beyond style, the foundation of effective leadership lies in trust. Leaders who foster trust within their teams often find themselves at the helm of more engaged, collaborative, and committed groups. Power, an intrinsic aspect of leadership, pertains to the ability to influence. How this power is employed - to control, to manipulate, or to inspire - has broad ramifications on the organizational milieu.

Lastly, politics, or the tactical use of influence for specific outcomes, is a reality in most organizational settings. While the term 'office politics' often carries negative connotations, when used judiciously, it can catalyze positive change and innovation. Leaders, however, need to remain alert, ensuring that politics doesn't breed division or prompt unethical behaviors.

Organizational Culture and Climate

In the grand theater of organizational life, if strategies, structures, and systems are the visible sets and stages, then organizational culture is the invisible yet palpable ambiance that pervades every act and scene. It's the underlying ethos that dictates how employees interact, make decisions, and perceive their roles within the larger narrative of the organization.

Organizational culture signifies the shared values, beliefs, and practices that guide the actions and behaviors of members of an organization. It's much like an iceberg: while certain aspects, like dress codes or office layouts, are immediately visible, the vast majority, encompassing values, norms, and unwritten rules, remain submerged, felt but not always seen.

A myriad of factors come together to shape and mold organizational culture. Leadership, undeniably, plays a pivotal role. The vision and values leaders espouse, the behaviors they reward, and the stories they recount all play a part in shaping the cultural fabric. Historical legacies, too, leave their imprint. The origins of an organization, past challenges it's surmounted, and milestones it's achieved can influence its cultural leanings. Additionally, strategies and objectives, especially when consistently communicated and pursued, can mold the culture. For instance, a company emphasizing rapid innovation might cultivate a culture that values risk-taking and fast decision-making.

Understanding the dynamics of culture becomes even more critical when we consider its relationship with organizational behavior. A positive, inclusive culture can spur employees to greater heights, boosting collaboration, innovation, and overall productivity. On the other hand, a toxic culture can stifle creativity, breed mistrust, and hinder performance. The ripple effects of culture echo through every corridor and cubicle, impacting job satisfaction, turnover rates, and even the bottom line.

The overarching climate of an organization - the collective perceptions and attitudes of its members - often mirrors its culture. While culture delves into shared values and norms, climate is about how employees feel regarding the organizational environment. A healthy organizational climate, nurtured by a positive culture, can be a powerful catalyst for improved performance, employee satisfaction, and retention.

Organizational culture and climate are not mere HR buzzwords. They're critical, intertwined entities that have a tangible impact on the performance and health of an organization. Leaders and decision-makers who prioritize understanding and shaping their culture are making an investment that will yield dividends in terms of employee morale, innovation, and overall success.

Communication in Organizations

Communication, often termed the lifeblood of an organization, is the linchpin holding together the vast machinery of corporate entities. In an organizational context, it traverses a wide spectrum from the exchange of ideas during a brainstorming session to official memos circulated across departments. Its impact reverberates through the organization's hierarchy, influencing decision-making, collaboration, and the overall rhythm of operations.

One of the primary facets of communication is its modality. Verbal communication, encompassing face-to-face discussions, phone calls, and virtual meetings, offers immediacy and often aids in building rapport among team members. However, the reliance on spoken words also implies the risk of misinterpretations, especially in the absence of supporting visual cues. Non-verbal communication, which includes body language, gestures, and even silence, can sometimes convey more than words. It plays a subconscious yet critical role in interpersonal interactions, offering cues about emotions, intent, and receptiveness. Written communication, spanning emails, reports, and official documents, provides clarity and permanence. It ensures that information is documented, yet it's imperative to be precise and unambiguous, given the absence of tone and facial expressions.

As vital as communication is, organizations frequently grapple with barriers that impede its effectiveness. These barriers could be physical, such as geographical distance between teams, or technological, like outdated communication tools. But more often than not, the challenges are more intangible. Hierarchical barriers, where information gets filtered or distorted as it moves up or down the ladder, or cultural barriers, where differences in language, values, or norms lead to misunderstandings, can significantly stymie effective communication.

Considering the importance of communication, enhancing it becomes a strategic imperative. Encouraging open dialogues across hierarchies can foster an environment of trust and collaboration. Cross-departmental meetings can bridge information gaps, ensuring that teams aren't working in silos. Training sessions can equip employees with the tools and techniques to communicate effectively, be it through active listening or effective presentation skills. Moreover, leveraging technology, from collaboration platforms to video conferencing tools, can streamline communication and ensure that teams, whether co-located or dispersed geographically, remain connected.

Decision Making and Negotiation

Decision making in an organizational context is akin to navigating a ship through intricate waters. It's a process that involves evaluating various courses of action, foreseeing potential obstacles, and choosing a direction that aligns with the organization's objectives. While individual decisions might seem straightforward, organizational decisions encompass a multitude of variables – stakeholder interests, financial implications, market dynamics, and long-term strategic goals, to name a few.

The decision-making process in organizations often commences with the identification of a problem or an opportunity. This is followed by gathering relevant information and analyzing potential solutions or courses of action. Once a range of alternatives is mapped out, they're evaluated in terms of feasibility, impact, and alignment with organizational goals. The final step involves making a choice, implementing it, and then reviewing its effectiveness post-implementation.

This seemingly systematic process is fraught with challenges. Cognitive biases, such as confirmation bias (favoring information that aligns with our pre-existing beliefs) or anchoring (relying heavily on the first piece of information encountered), can skew the decision-making process. Organizational politics, where different departments or stakeholders have competing interests, can lead to gridlocks. Additionally, the sheer volume of data available in today's digital age can lead to analysis paralysis, where decision-makers find it hard to make a choice due to being overwhelmed with information.

Closely intertwined with decision-making is the art of negotiation. Whether it's hammering out a deal with a vendor, resolving conflicts within teams, or aligning disparate departments towards a common goal, negotiation is an indispensable skill in the corporate toolbox. Effective negotiation isn't about "winning" but finding a mutually beneficial solution. It involves understanding the interests of all parties involved, effective communication to express and understand concerns, and a judicious mix of collaboration and compromise.

Various techniques and strategies can enhance negotiation outcomes. Active listening, where negotiators genuinely try to understand the other party's perspective, can build trust. Preparing thoroughly, by understanding one's Best Alternative To a Negotiated Agreement (BATNA), can provide leverage. Additionally, separating people from the problem can ensure that negotiations remain objective and don't devolve into personal conflicts.

Both decision-making and negotiation are about charting a course through the intricate landscape of organizational dynamics. They require a combination of analytical acumen, interpersonal skills, and a clear vision of the broader organizational goals. When executed effectively, they can steer organizations through challenges and towards success, ensuring resilience and adaptability in a constantly evolving business environment.

Change and Stress Management

In the ever-evolving landscape of business, change is the only constant. Organizations must adapt to shifts in the market, technological advancements, and evolving consumer preferences to remain relevant and competitive. Yet, despite its inevitability, change often meets resistance. The reasons can range from a natural human aversion to the unknown to concerns about the tangible impacts on roles, responsibilities, and organizational hierarchies.

Understanding organizational change necessitates a grasp of its various facets. At its core, change can either be reactive, responding to external factors like market changes or proactive, stemming from internal strategic decisions. Whether it's adopting a new technology, venturing into a new market, restructuring, or undergoing a cultural transformation, the implications of organizational change are vast. These alterations not only affect the day-to-day operations but also influence the broader organizational ethos, mission, and vision.

Resistance to change can manifest in various ways, from overt opposition and skepticism to subtle foot-dragging. Such resistance isn't always negative; it can signal valid concerns that need addressing. To navigate these choppy waters, effective change management strategies are crucial. These can include clear communication about the reasons for the change, its benefits, and its implications. Engaging stakeholders early, incorporating their feedback, and involving them in the change process can foster a sense of ownership and reduce resistance. Training and support mechanisms, both during and post the change, can further ease the transition.

Even with the most seamless change management processes, stress is an inevitable byproduct. The uncertainty that change brings, coupled with the pressures of adapting to new systems or norms, can be overwhelming. Furthermore, in today's fast-paced business world, stressors aren't limited to organizational changes. Tight deadlines, high expectations, interpersonal conflicts, and the challenge of maintaining a work-life balance can all contribute to stress.

The impact of stress on organizational behavior is profound. It can lead to decreased productivity, increased absenteeism, health issues, and even burnout. Recognizing this, organizations are increasingly prioritizing stress management not just as a wellness initiative, but as a strategic imperative. Techniques for stress management range from fostering a positive work environment and promoting work-life balance to providing resources like counseling and relaxation workshops. Encouraging regular breaks, flexible working conditions, and promoting open communication where employees feel heard and validated can also mitigate stress levels.

In the intricate tapestry of business, organizational behavior stands out as a pivotal thread, weaving together individual aspirations, group dynamics, and overarching organizational goals. As we reflect upon its expansive landscape, it's evident that organizational behavior is not a static discipline; it's perpetually evolving. The factors that shaped organizational behaviors decades ago differ significantly from today's influencers, be it the rise of digital communication, the gig economy, the push for greater inclusivity, or the global nature of modern businesses.

Looking ahead, several trends and challenges beckon. The increasing integration of artificial intelligence and machine learning into workplaces, for instance, will redefine roles and decision-making processes. Remote and flexible work, accelerated by global events like the COVID-19 pandemic, will influence team dynamics, communication, and leadership styles. As organizations become more global, the intricacies of navigating diverse cultural nuances will become even more pronounced. Additionally, the growing emphasis on sustainability and social responsibility will further shape organizational missions, values, and behaviors.

Yet, amidst this flux, one truth remains unyielding: the profound importance of understanding and optimizing organizational behavior. At its heart, a business is about people. And to drive success – whether measured in terms of profitability, innovation, or societal impact – understanding the motivations, behaviors, and aspirations of those people is crucial. Organizational behavior offers a lens through which we can better comprehend this human dimension of business. By continually refining our understanding, adapting to new challenges, and fostering environments where every individual feels valued and empowered, organizations can not only achieve their immediate goals but also ensure enduring success in the future.

Exercise 6: "Your OB Journey Map"

Objective: Delve into the world of organizational behavior (OB) by piecing together its various components. By the end of this exercise, you'll have a holistic picture of OB's intricacies and its importance in organizational settings.

Materials You'll Need:
- ☐ A set of pre-made index cards. Each card holds a unique term or concept related to organizational behavior.
- ☐ A whiteboard and markers.

Setting the Stage:
- ☐ You'll start by joining a small group of 4-5 fellow students.
- ☐ Each group gets a unique set of index cards filled with OB terms and concepts.

Your Initial Discussions: Spend about 10 minutes within your group, discussing and understanding the OB concepts you've been handed. This is your time to question, analyze, and truly grasp these terms.

Mix and Match: Once you've had a robust discussion, it's time to shuffle up. Join a new group with students who had a different set of terms. Each of you will introduce one OB term or concept you've previously discussed, explaining its nuances and how it might interconnect with others.

Mapping Your Understanding: As the discussion unfolds, one representative from each group will draw these concepts on the whiteboard, linking related terms. Watch as the whiteboard turns into a web of interconnected OB principles.

Collective Insight:

- [ ] With everyone's input on the board, it's time for a collective discussion. You might ponder:
- [ ] Did any connections between concepts surprise you?
- [ ] Which areas of OB, according to your map, seem most influential?
- [ ] Can you recall any real-life instances where these OB concepts played out?

Reflect and Relate: To conclude, ponder on why it's essential to understand these interconnections. Think about how a change in one OB area might ripple through and affect others.

Through this exercise, you'll experience firsthand how multifaceted organizational behavior is. By weaving different OB components together, you're better preparing yourself to handle and navigate complex organizational challenges. It's not just about understanding the individual elements, but seeing the bigger picture. Enjoy the journey!

Chapter 7: Leadership Development

The journey of leadership development is as much a psychological one as it is about acquiring skills or knowledge. In the intricate dance of leading and following, the mind plays a pivotal role, influencing perceptions, decisions, actions, and reactions. Delving into the realm of leadership from a psychological perspective illuminates the deeper undercurrents that shape leadership trajectories, from the nascent stages of potential identification to the continual growth nurtured through education and mentorship.

First and foremost, the act of identifying potential leaders is steeped in psychology. It's not just about recognizing overt traits or exemplary performance. Instead, it delves deep into understanding cognitive capacities, emotional intelligence, intrinsic motivations, and the myriad other psychological factors that signify a budding leader. These individuals often possess a unique alchemy of self-awareness, resilience, and vision, driving them to chart unfamiliar territories.

Following identification, the arena of training and education comes to the fore. While it's essential to impart relevant skills and knowledge, the psychological aspect of this training is paramount. It is here that potential leaders confront their limitations, face their fears, and learn the art of resilience. Educational modules designed with a psychological lens focus on self-reflection, self-awareness, and the cultivation of an empathetic, growth-oriented mindset. They challenge participants to not only grasp leadership theories but also to introspect, understand their mental frameworks, and be willing to evolve.

Mentorship and coaching holds profound psychological significance. A mentor, with their reservoir of experience, offers not just guidance but also a mirror, reflecting both strengths and areas for growth. Coaching, on the other hand, is a journey inward, often nudging individuals to confront deep-seated beliefs, biases, and barriers. The coach facilitates a transformative process, enabling individuals to tap into their psychological depths, harness their strengths, and work on their limitations.

Chapter 7 seeks to elucidate the profound psychological dimensions of leadership development. From the initial stages of spotting potential to the ongoing journey of growth through education, mentorship, and coaching, the chapter underscores the inextricable link between psychology and leadership. Through this exploration, readers will gain a deeper appreciation of the mental and emotional landscapes that mold effective, empathetic, and visionary leaders.

Identifying the Potential Leader in Ourselves

Discovering the potential leader within is a transformative journey that demands introspection, self-awareness, and a commitment to growth. Leadership is not exclusively about leading others; it begins with leading oneself. Before we can effectively guide, inspire, or influence others, we must first understand and command our own internal world. This self-leadership lays the foundation for outward leadership.

One of the first steps in recognizing our leadership potential is acknowledging our unique strengths. Every individual possesses a set of skills, talents, and abilities that can be channeled towards leadership. By reflecting on past experiences, challenges overcome, and successes achieved, one can glean insights into personal strengths. These reflections often reveal patterns of resilience, problem-solving, innovation, or the ability to inspire and mobilize others.

Alongside strengths, it's equally important to confront our vulnerabilities and areas of improvement. This isn't about self-criticism but about fostering a growth mindset. Recognizing areas where we can evolve or enhance our skills is crucial for leadership development. Potential leaders are not those who are flawless but those who are continually learning and growing.

Emotional intelligence plays a pivotal role in this journey of self-discovery. It's not just about understanding our emotions but also about recognizing how they impact our decisions, interactions, and leadership style. By cultivating emotional self-awareness, we can better navigate the complexities of interpersonal relationships, a key facet of leadership.

Seeking feedback is invaluable in this explorative process. Constructive feedback, whether from peers, mentors, or team members, provides an external perspective on our leadership style, approach, and potential. It offers insights into areas of excellence and those that require attention.

A fundamental aspect of identifying the potential leader within revolves around vision. Potential leaders often harbor a vision or purpose that transcends their individual goals. This vision fuels their passion, drives their actions, and resonates with others. Reflecting on what truly matters to us, the change we wish to see, or the legacy we aspire to leave can offer profound insights into our leadership potential.

Vision is an integral attribute of potential leaders. It's more than just a fleeting idea or a momentary aspiration; it's a deeply rooted sense of purpose that guides every decision, every action, and every interaction. Such vision is not restricted by the constraints of the present but stretches the imagination to see possibilities, opportunities, and the potential for meaningful change in the future.

When one possesses a clear vision, it becomes a beacon that illuminates their path, helping them navigate through uncertainties and challenges. It's this vision that makes potential leaders stand out. They aren't merely reacting to situations or drifting along with prevailing trends. Instead, they are proactive, charting a course based on their deeply held beliefs and values.

A vision is often contagious. When articulated with conviction and passion, it has the power to inspire and mobilize those around. It creates a shared sense of purpose, forging bonds between the leader and their team, making the collective endeavor far more meaningful. It's no wonder that the most transformative leaders in history, from Nelson Mandela to Steve Jobs, were visionaries in their own right. Their visions were not mere dreams but compelling narratives that galvanized action and brought about significant change.

Reflecting on one's personal vision entails asking profound questions about one's aspirations for the future, the values that are non-negotiable, and the kind of impact one desires to have on their community, organization, or even the world. Such reflection helps crystallize thoughts and provides clarity on the path ahead. As potential leaders sharpen their vision, they equip themselves with one of the most potent tools in leadership, setting the stage for influence, impact, and transformation.

Personal Mission Statement

Developing a personal mission is akin to crafting a compass for one's life journey. It acts as a guiding principle, helping to align actions with values, and providing a consistent direction amidst the ever-shifting landscapes of personal and professional life.

A personal mission transcends daily tasks and goals. While objectives and targets might change based on circumstances, a personal mission remains steadfast, providing a sense of purpose and stability. It addresses fundamental questions like, "Why do I do what I do?" and "What greater purpose do I serve through my actions?" By answering these queries, individuals gain a clearer understanding of their role in the larger tapestry of life.

The process of crafting a personal mission often begins with introspection. It requires delving deep into one's values, passions, strengths, and desires. What are the activities that ignite a spark within you? Which accomplishments have given you the most satisfaction? What are the values you refuse to compromise on, no matter the situation? These introspective explorations lay the foundation for a mission that truly resonates.

Once the groundwork of introspection is laid, the next step is articulation. Transforming these insights into a succinct statement can be challenging but profoundly rewarding. A well-phrased personal mission statement should be both aspirational, pointing towards a higher purpose, and actionable, providing clear directives that can guide daily decisions and behaviors.

A personal mission isn't set in stone; it's organic and can evolve as one grows and gains more life experiences. As priorities shift and perspectives broaden, it's beneficial to revisit and, if necessary, recalibrate the mission statement to ensure it remains aligned with one's evolving self.

Developing a personal mission is not just an exercise in self-awareness; it's a commitment to living with intentionality. It's about recognizing one's agency in shaping their destiny, ensuring that every step taken is aligned with a broader purpose, and consistently striving to lead a life of significance and impact.

Training and Education

At its core, training and education are about nurturing the psychological foundations that underpin effective leadership. To truly grasp the essence of leadership, one must delve into the intricate interplay between cognitive processes, emotional intelligence, behavioral tendencies, and societal influences.

The psychology of leadership underscores the importance of self-awareness. Training programs often begin with introspective exercises, designed to help individuals recognize their inherent strengths, weaknesses, biases, and motivations. By understanding oneself better, aspiring leaders are better positioned to empathize with others, make informed decisions, and adapt their leadership style to suit different situations.

But self-awareness is just the tip of the iceberg. The psychological landscape of leadership extends to understanding others. Educational programs emphasize the importance of social cognition, helping leaders grasp how individuals think, feel, and make decisions within group settings. Such insights are invaluable when it comes to team dynamics, conflict resolution, and motivation.

The role of emotions in leadership cannot be understated. Emotional intelligence, a concept popularized by psychologist Daniel Goleman, is central to modern leadership training. Leaders are taught to recognize, understand, and manage their emotions while also being attuned to the emotions of those around them. This not only aids in fostering positive interpersonal relationships but also in navigating the complex emotional terrains of organizational life.

In addition to intrapersonal and interpersonal dynamics, leadership education delves into the broader organizational psychology. It encompasses understanding organizational cultures, dynamics, and the subtle nuances that influence group behavior. Such insights equip leaders to drive change, foster innovation, and build cohesive teams that share a unified vision.

Contemporary leadership education also recognizes the importance of continuous learning. The rapidly changing global landscape, marked by technological advancements and shifting socio-cultural dynamics, necessitates leaders to be lifelong learners. This adaptability, rooted in a growth mindset as elucidated by psychologist Carol Dweck, is a key focus of modern leadership training.

Incorporating these psychological elements into leadership training and education ensures a holistic development approach. It goes beyond the mechanics of leading and delves into the deeper realms of influencing, inspiring, and making a lasting impact. After all, true leadership is as much about understanding the human psyche as it is about strategy and execution.

Mentorship and Coaching

Mentorship and coaching are invaluable tools in the leadership development journey. Both approaches serve as catalysts, helping individuals bridge the gap between their current capabilities and their leadership potential. While they often intersect, mentorship and coaching have distinct characteristics and purposes, deeply rooted in the psychology of leadership.

Mentorship is essentially a relationship, often long-term, between a seasoned expert (the mentor) and a less experienced individual (the mentee). This relationship is built on mutual respect, trust, and a shared goal of personal and professional growth. The mentor, leveraging their experience and insights, provides guidance, advice, and resources to the mentee. The mentee, in turn, brings fresh perspectives, questions, and a zeal to learn. This symbiotic relationship facilitates not just skill acquisition but also a deeper understanding of oneself and one's professional landscape.

Psychologically, mentorship is pivotal in shaping an individual's self-efficacy and confidence. As mentees navigate the challenges of their roles, having a mentor provides reassurance, affirmation, and constructive feedback. Such interactions not only build competence but also instill a belief in one's abilities. Moreover, mentors often serve as role models, offering tangible examples of leadership in action. Observing and interacting with someone who epitomizes effective leadership can profoundly influence one's leadership philosophy and style.

Delving deeper into the psychological impact of mentorship, we find that it plays an essential role in molding the foundational beliefs an individual holds about their abilities, commonly referred to as self-efficacy. Albert Bandura, a renowned psychologist, posited that self-efficacy is shaped by four main sources: mastery experiences, vicarious experiences, verbal persuasion, and physiological responses. Mentorship touches on each of these aspects.

Mastery experiences are the instances where an individual succeeds at a task or overcomes an obstacle. When mentees face challenges, mentors guide them, providing strategies and insights. As mentees employ these strategies and experience successes, their belief in their capability strengthens. This cycle of challenge, guidance, action, and success gradually builds a robust sense of self-efficacy.

Vicarious experiences come from seeing others, especially those we deem similar to us, succeed using effort and skill. Mentors, through their lived experiences, share stories of their challenges, failures, and eventual successes. These narratives offer mentees a roadmap, showing them that success is attainable. Seeing a mentor, whom a mentee respects and identifies with, traverse challenges successfully, instills a belief in the mentee that they too can achieve similar feats.

Verbal persuasion involves others expressing belief in our capabilities. A mentor's affirmations and reassurances can be potent. When a mentor, with their wealth of experience, communicates their belief in a mentee's potential, it carries weight. This external validation, especially when coming from a respected figure, reinforces the mentee's self-belief.

Physiological responses pertain to the emotional states individuals experience as they face challenges. Fear, stress, or anxiety can erode self-efficacy. However, a mentor's presence acts as a stabilizing force. Knowing that there's someone to turn to, someone who has perhaps faced similar emotions and overcome them, can mitigate the intensity of these negative emotions.

The role of a mentor extends beyond being a guide; they often serve as a mirror, reflecting both the strengths and areas of growth for the mentee. Their feedback, grounded in care and genuine interest in the mentee's development, helps shape not just skills but also character.

The mentor's role as a role model is crucial. Leaders often craft their leadership style based on a blend of their values, experiences, and the role models they've had. Interacting with a mentor provides a live demonstration of leadership principles in action. Whether it's the way a mentor handles conflict, communicates, or makes decisions, each interaction offers lessons. By observing and internalizing these lessons, mentees can refine their leadership philosophy, ensuring it's both effective and authentic.

Coaching, on the other hand, is more structured and is often time-bound. It involves a professional coach working with an individual, focusing on specific goals or challenges. Unlike mentorship, where the mentor often speaks from their experience, coaching is more about facilitating self-discovery. Coaches employ techniques like questioning, reflection, and feedback to help individuals gain clarity, devise action plans, and overcome obstacles.

Coaching, in its essence, can be likened to a collaborative exploration. It dives deep into the coachee's aspirations, capabilities, beliefs, and challenges. The coach's primary role isn't to instruct or advise, but rather to guide this exploration, ensuring it's both structured and enlightening.

A fundamental distinction between coaching and other forms of professional guidance is its emphasis on the present and future, rather than the past. While therapy often delves into past experiences to understand and heal, coaching is firmly rooted in the present moment, leveraging it as a launchpad for future aspirations. This forward-looking approach aligns perfectly with leadership development, focusing on honing skills, rectifying behaviors, and charting growth trajectories.

One of the hallmarks of coaching is its commitment to self-discovery. Coaches believe in the inherent potential and wisdom of their coachees. Through thought-provoking questions and deep reflections, coaches challenge coachees to tap into this reservoir of potential. This process isn't just about achieving set goals but also about fostering self-awareness. Such awareness is pivotal for leadership as it aids in decision-making, relationship-building, and personal growth.

The psychological underpinnings of coaching emphasize the importance of creating a safe, non-judgmental space. In such an environment, coachees feel empowered to express themselves authentically, delve into their vulnerabilities, and confront their limitations. This psychological safety, coupled with the coach's unbiased perspective, often leads to breakthrough realizations.

Another integral facet of coaching is accountability. While a coach facilitates self-discovery, they also ensure that the coachee remains committed to their action plans. This balance between exploration and execution is vital. By setting clear milestones and regularly reviewing progress, coaches ensure that coachees don't just gain insights but also translate them into tangible actions. This emphasis on action and accountability often accelerates growth, leading to measurable outcomes in a relatively short span.

Coaching embodies the principle of adaptability. Given its structured nature, sessions are often tailored to address specific challenges or goals. Whether it's a leader grappling with decision-making, team dynamics, or personal productivity, coaching sessions can be designed to address these unique needs, ensuring relevance and impact.

In a world where leadership roles are continually evolving, demanding not just expertise but also emotional intelligence, adaptability, and resilience, coaching emerges as a powerful tool. By fostering self-awareness, encouraging proactive action, and focusing on continuous growth, coaching aligns perfectly with the demands of modern leadership, ensuring leaders are not just effective but also emotionally and psychologically attuned.

From a psychological perspective, coaching hinges on the premise that individuals, when given the right environment and tools, can unearth solutions and insights within themselves. It taps into intrinsic motivation, fostering a sense of ownership and accountability. Moreover, coaching emphasizes the importance of self-awareness and introspection. As individuals dissect their thoughts, emotions, and behaviors under the coach's guidance, they gain deeper insights into their leadership style, strengths, and areas of improvement.

Coaching provides a safe space for vulnerability. Leaders, especially in high-stakes environments, may find it challenging to express doubts, fears, or perceived inadequacies. A coach offers a non-judgmental environment, encouraging open dialogue, and fostering growth through self-reflection.

Mentorship and coaching are more than mere developmental tools. They are journeys of self-discovery, resilience-building, and continuous learning. Through these processes, individuals not only sharpen their leadership skills but also evolve psychologically, becoming more attuned to themselves and the world around them. As the landscape of leadership continues to evolve, the significance of mentorship and coaching, with their deeply psychological foundations, remains paramount.

Exercise 7: Developing Your Personal Mission Statement

Objective: To help you reflect upon and articulate your personal mission in life. This exercise will guide you in understanding your core values, aspirations, and how you envision your role in the larger context of society.

Duration: 45 minutes

Materials Needed:
- ☐ Notebook or paper
- ☐ Pens or pencils
- ☐ A quiet room with seating arrangement conducive for personal reflection

Instructions:

Warm-up (5 minutes): Begin by asking yourself: "If I were to describe my life's purpose in one sentence, what would it be?" Jot down the first thoughts that come to your mind. This is just a warm-up, so don't overthink it.

Reflection (10 minutes): Close your eyes and take a deep breath. Reflect on moments in your life when you felt the most fulfilled, proud, or truly alive. What were you doing? Who were you with? What value were you adding?

Listing Core Values (10 minutes): Write down five core values that resonate with you the most. These values should reflect who you are and what matters most to you. For instance, some might choose values like compassion, resilience, authenticity, or integrity.

Drafting Your Mission Statement (15 minutes): Based on your reflections and core values, start drafting a personal mission statement. This statement should encapsulate what you stand for, what you aim to achieve in life, and how you want to make a difference. Remember, this is a draft. Your mission might evolve over time, and that's okay. The aim is to have a starting point that provides clarity and direction.

Sharing (Optional, 5 minutes): If you're comfortable, share your mission statement with a partner or small group. Listening to others can provide insights and inspiration for your own mission.

Debrief: At the end of the exercise, have a short discussion on the experience. Did you discover something new about yourself? Was articulating a mission challenging? Did others' mission statements inspire or resonate?

Chapter 8: Ethics and the Psychology of Leadership

There's a vital dimension that often becomes the keystone of truly influential and enduring leaders: ethics. Ethical leadership isn't just a lofty ideal; it's a tangible, actionable paradigm that intersects profoundly with the psychology of leading and being led. In an era where the quest for power, profits, and prominence can sometimes overshadow integrity and authenticity, how do leaders navigate the murky waters of ethical dilemmas? How do they foster a culture that places ethical considerations at the forefront of decisions? And how do these leaders, rooted in moral fiber, influence the larger organizational ecosystem?

This chapter seeks to delve into the very psyche of ethical leadership. Beginning with the challenges leaders face in the ever-evolving landscapes of corporate, political, and social realms, we examine the intricacies of what it means to lead ethically. Ethical quandaries are seldom black and white; they exist in the greys, demanding nuanced understanding, reflection, and often, the courage to tread the path less traveled.

But it isn't enough to simply recognize these challenges. Leaders play a monumental role in shaping the ethos of their organizations. Hence, understanding how to build and nurture ethical cultures becomes paramount. It's not just about personal morality; it's about creating an environment where every stakeholder, from the newest recruit to the senior-most executive, internalizes and exemplifies these values.

At the heart of ethical leadership lies the intricate process of moral decision-making. When faced with dilemmas, how do leaders make choices that align with their ethical compass? How does the psychology of morality intersect with leadership strategies and behaviors?

Our aim is to not only elucidate concepts but also provide tools, insights, and reflections to help emerging and established leaders alike champion the cause of ethics in their leadership journey. After all, in the words of Albert Schweitzer, "Example is not the main thing in influencing others; it is the only thing."

Ethical and Moral Challenges in Leadership

In the complex world of leadership, ethical challenges aren't rare occurrences—they are daily tests of a leader's moral compass and integrity. With globalization, rapid technological advancements, and evolving societal expectations, leaders today find themselves in a crucible of dilemmas that demand not only strategic acumen but also deep ethical introspection.

A primary challenge facing many leaders is balancing the pursuit of organizational goals with ethical considerations. Whether it's about achieving quarterly targets, appeasing stakeholders, or gaining a competitive edge, leaders often find themselves under immense pressure. Succumbing to this pressure might tempt some to bypass ethical norms, justifying such actions as necessary for the "greater good" of the organization. But in reality, such shortcuts can undermine the long-term health of an entity, both in terms of reputation and sustainable success.

Another predicament leaders frequently encounter is managing conflicting interests. A decision that benefits one group might adversely affect another. For example, a corporate decision to downsize may improve bottom-line efficiency but at the cost of employee well-being and morale. Leaders must weigh these outcomes, ensuring that decisions, even if tough, are made transparently and ethically.

Cultural diversity in globalized workspaces presents yet another ethical dimension. Leaders must be acutely aware of and sensitive to cultural nuances and moral frameworks that might differ from their own. What is considered an acceptable leadership practice in one culture might be viewed as unethical in another. This requires leaders to be culturally literate and adaptable, always aiming for a universal standard of ethical behavior.

Transparency and honesty also pose challenges in the realm of ethical leadership. In an age of information overload, leaders must be judicious about what they communicate, ensuring that transparency doesn't morph into oversharing, and discretion doesn't become deceit.

The stakes are high, but the rewards of ethical leadership are manifold. Ethical leaders not only safeguard their organizations from potential pitfalls but also inspire trust, loyalty, and respect among their followers. As they navigate these challenges, leaders sculpt the very ethos of their organizations, laying the foundation for a legacy rooted in integrity and honor.

Diving into the core of leadership ethics, we encounter the intricate arena of moral decision making. It is a realm where leaders face multifaceted situations that demand more than just business acumen or technical know-how. These situations require a synthesis of values, principles, and a commitment to doing what's right—even when it's not the easiest path.

Every day, leaders are bombarded with choices. Some are straightforward, while others are imbued with moral implications that can have lasting impacts on individuals, teams, and entire organizations. Decisions related to layoffs, business partnerships, product recalls, or even corporate social responsibility initiatives all carry ethical weight. Making the right choice in such scenarios often means delving deep into one's moral compass, evaluating the potential harm and benefit of each option, and perhaps most importantly, being willing to face the consequences of that choice.

The process of moral decision making often starts with recognizing that a particular decision carries ethical significance. This recognition is followed by gathering all relevant information, forecasting potential outcomes, and consulting with trusted advisors or mentors. However, what sets moral decisions apart is the next step: introspection. Leaders must reflect upon their values, consider the broader implications of the decision for all stakeholders involved, and envision the long-term repercussions.

Psychologically, the act of making moral decisions can be taxing. It invokes cognitive dissonance—a state where one grapples with conflicting attitudes, beliefs, or behaviors. Leaders might feel torn between their personal beliefs and external pressures or between short-term gains and long-term values. Navigating this dissonance and arriving at a decision that aligns with one's ethical principles is the hallmark of genuine leadership.

The contemporary landscape of instant news and social media adds another layer to the decision-making process. Leaders are now under constant scrutiny, with their decisions, actions, and even inactions dissected and debated publicly. This transparency amplifies the importance of moral decisiveness and consistency in leadership.

Moral decision making is an ongoing journey for leaders, one that requires courage, reflection, and an unwavering commitment to ethical integrity. It's about acknowledging the gravity of the role a leader plays and understanding that their decisions echo far beyond boardroom walls, shaping cultures, influencing perceptions, and ultimately determining the legacy they leave behind.

Building Ethical Cultures

Establishing an ethical culture within organizations goes beyond simply adhering to laws and regulations. It entails fostering an environment where principles of fairness, integrity, and transparency are embedded in every decision and action. This culture influences not just the macro decisions of the company, such as its strategic direction, but also the micro decisions that each employee makes daily. An ethical culture serves as the organization's moral compass, guiding behaviors even in situations where the path might seem ambiguous.

The importance of such a culture cannot be overstated. Ethical organizations are not only seen as trustworthy in the eyes of their stakeholders, but they also often outperform competitors in the long run. This stems from a variety of factors: employees feel proud to be associated with such organizations, leading to increased engagement and reduced turnover; customers and partners prefer to associate with businesses that uphold high ethical standards, ensuring sustained revenues and collaborative opportunities; and in times of crises, these organizations garner more support and understanding from the public and stakeholders, given their track record of ethical behavior.

Leaders play a pivotal role in shaping and promoting this ethical culture. Their actions, more than their words, set the tone for the entire organization. When leaders prioritize ethics, they send a clear message that ethical behavior is not just encouraged but expected. By leading with integrity, transparency, and fairness, they not only foster trust within their teams but also inspire others to uphold these same values. Furthermore, leaders have the responsibility to ensure that the organization's structures, processes, and incentives support ethical decision-making. This might include establishing clear ethical guidelines, investing in training, or setting up systems for anonymous reporting of unethical behaviors.

Promoting an ethical culture is not a one-time task. It requires consistent effort, vigilance, and adaptability. As businesses evolve and face new challenges, their approach to ethics also needs to adapt. Leaders must remain at the forefront of this evolution, continually assessing and reinforcing the ethical culture of their organizations, and ensuring it aligns with the ever-changing global landscape.

An ethical culture, much like a thriving ecosystem, consists of various components that interact, reinforce, and sustain one another. Without one, the whole system could falter. When we talk about creating and nurturing an ethical culture within an organization, it's crucial to understand these fundamental components and how they interplay.

Clear ethical standards and guidelines form the bedrock of an ethical culture. Without a well-defined set of standards, employees might find themselves at sea, unsure of the right course of action in complex situations. These standards need to be comprehensive, covering not just legal compliance but also moral principles like honesty, integrity, and respect. More than just a list of do's and don'ts, these guidelines should inspire employees to strive for higher standards. They should act as a beacon, guiding individuals through the murkier waters of ethical dilemmas.

Open communication channels play a significant role in breathing life into these standards. Employees, regardless of their position in the organizational hierarchy, should feel comfortable discussing ethical concerns without fear of retribution. Leaders and managers should actively foster an environment where such conversations are encouraged, be it through formal channels like town hall meetings or more informal platforms like team discussions. Such open dialogues not only help in addressing immediate concerns but also instill a sense of collective ownership of the organization's ethical stance.

Even with clear standards and open communication, navigating ethical challenges can be daunting. This is where training and resources for ethical decision-making come into play. By investing in regular training sessions, workshops, and seminars, organizations empower their employees with the tools and frameworks needed to tackle ethical dilemmas head-on. These training sessions can be complemented with resources like case studies, articles, or even dedicated helplines where employees can seek guidance. Together, these resources act as a support system, ensuring that employees are never left to grapple with ethical challenges on their own.

In stitching together these components, an organization creates a robust tapestry of ethical culture. It's a culture where moral principles are not just words on paper but are lived and breathed by every member, every day. And as the organization grows and evolves, this ethical foundation ensures that it remains rooted in its core values, always striving for the greater good.

Leadership is not just about setting a direction and guiding a team towards a shared vision; it's also about defining and upholding the moral compass of an organization. The role of leaders in cultivating and reinforcing an ethical culture is both profound and multifaceted. Their actions and decisions set the tone for the organization, creating ripples that influence every level of the workforce.

At the forefront of ethical leadership is the principle of leading by example. The age-old adage of "walking the talk" holds profound truth here. Leaders cannot merely preach ethics; they must embody them in their actions, decisions, and interactions. When employees see their leaders making tough decisions that align with ethical values, even when it might not be the most profitable or easiest path, they gain confidence in the organization's commitment to its principles. This embodiment of values serves as a powerful testament, far more impactful than any written code of conduct.

Creating an ethical culture goes beyond just setting an example; it also requires fostering an environment conducive to ethical discussions and reflections. Leaders should actively encourage their team members to voice concerns, share dilemmas, and seek guidance when faced with ethical quandaries. This can be achieved through regular team meetings focused on ethical case studies, open forums where employees can share and discuss real-life scenarios they've encountered, or even by leaders sharing their own experiences and the ethical challenges they've faced. These discussions not only provide clarity but also help in building a collective ethical consciousness.

Recognizing and rewarding ethical behavior is another pivotal role that leaders play. Just as achievements and performance are celebrated, instances where employees have demonstrated exceptional ethical judgment should be acknowledged and appreciated. Whether it's an employee who flagged a potential conflict of interest or a team that chose to prioritize quality over meeting a deadline, these actions need to be highlighted. By rewarding ethical behavior, leaders send a clear message about what's truly valued in the organization. It shifts the focus from short-term gains to long-term, sustainable success grounded in integrity.

Leaders are the torchbearers of an organization's ethical ethos. Through their actions, communication, and reinforcement mechanisms, they can either bolster a culture of integrity or erode it. In the intricate dance of organizational dynamics, their steps, more than anyone else's, determine the rhythm and direction of the organization's ethical journey.

In a rapidly changing world, it is essential for organizations to actively nurture and bolster their ethical cultures, ensuring that they remain relevant and robust. One-off training sessions or mere inclusion of ethics in the company handbook isn't sufficient. A proactive and multifaceted approach is needed to keep the ethical heartbeat of an organization strong and steady.

A crucial strategy is to conduct regular ethics audits and reviews. Just as financial audits assess an organization's monetary health, ethics audits delve deep into the company's moral fabric. By evaluating policies, practices, and employee perceptions, these audits identify potential vulnerabilities and areas of improvement. They serve as a mirror, reflecting the true state of the organization's ethical health and offering actionable insights.

Organizations should engage actively in community outreach and corporate social responsibility (CSR). Ethical grounding isn't limited to internal organizational practices; it extends to how a company interacts with the world at large. By investing time, resources, and expertise into community initiatives, organizations not only make a positive societal impact but also reinforce their commitment to ethical values. CSR projects resonate with both employees and consumers, showcasing the organization's dedication to causes larger than just profit.

Promoting diversity and inclusivity is paramount. Ethical dilemmas often exist in gray areas, where right and wrong aren't starkly demarcated. Having a diverse workforce ensures that these challenges are approached with varied perspectives, backgrounds, and thought processes. Inclusivity promotes a sense of belonging and ensures that all voices are heard, even when they might hold dissenting views. By fostering a culture where different viewpoints are valued and considered, organizations enrich their ethical discourse, making more informed and holistic decisions.

Building and maintaining an ethical culture is an ongoing journey, requiring consistent effort, introspection, and adaptability. However, with the right strategies in place, organizations can navigate the complex ethical landscape, ensuring that they remain beacons of integrity in the business world.

Exercise 8: Navigating Ethical Dilemmas – A Role-Play Activity

Objective: This exercise aims to immerse you in the complexities of workplace ethics. Through role-playing, you'll experience first-hand the challenges of navigating ethical dilemmas and understand the importance of promoting ethical cultures in organizations.

Materials Needed:
- ☐ Ethical dilemma case study handouts
- ☐ Role cards detailing your character's stance and perspective
- ☐ Whiteboard & markers for noting key points
- ☐ Feedback sheets for post-activity reflections

Introduction: First, let's remind ourselves why ethics is crucial. Ethical decisions in the workplace aren't always black and white. Sometimes, they're ambiguous and demand careful consideration.

Group Formation: You'll now be divided into small groups. Each group will receive a unique ethical dilemma case study. Within your group, each of you will be assigned a specific role related to the case (like a manager, employee, or HR representative).

Deliberation: Spend 20 minutes with your group discussing the ethical dilemma. Put yourself in the shoes of your assigned role. Think about their motivations, fears, and objectives. How would they view the situation? Decide together how you want to enact the scenario.

Performance: Once you've mapped out your approach, each group will present their role-play to the class, showcasing both the conflict and its resolution.

Discussion: After watching a presentation, let's engage in a constructive discussion. Share your observations about the role-play, discuss what resonated with you, and consider alternative approaches to the presented solution.

Reflection: Now, reflect on what you've learned. On your feedback sheet, answer questions like:
- Which scenario seemed most challenging to you, and why?
- How did you feel embodying a character facing an ethical challenge?
- What strategies or arguments seemed most convincing in these ethical discussions?

Debrief: To wrap up, we'll come together and discuss common themes, strategies, or realizations that emerged during the role-plays. We'll emphasize the value of open dialogue, empathy, and critical thinking when addressing ethical challenges in the workplace.

A Note to Remember: The ethical dilemmas in your handouts span various challenges you might face in the business world, from conflicts of interest to issues of confidentiality. Engage with them deeply, as understanding these challenges will be invaluable in your future careers.

Ethical Dilemma Case Study Handouts

Case Study 1: Confidentiality vs. Safety

You are a manager in a pharmaceutical company. A trusted employee confides in you that they accidentally compromised the results of a drug trial but has fixed it without notifying higher-ups. Reporting it would delay the drug's release by a year and might cost the company millions. What do you do?

Roles:

Manager
Trusted Employee
Co-worker who overheard the conversation

Case Study 2: Profit vs. Environmental Responsibility
You work in a manufacturing company. You discover a way to cut production costs by 30%, but it involves dumping untreated waste into nearby rivers. The waste is not illegal but could harm the ecosystem.

Roles:
CEO
Environmental Consultant
Local Community Member

Case Study 3: Personal Gain vs. Organizational Integrity
A vendor offers you tickets to an exclusive event if you choose their services over a competitor's, even though the competitor offers a slightly better deal for the company. Accepting gifts from vendors is against company policy.

Roles:
Employee being offered the tickets
Vendor
Colleague aware of the offer

Case Study 4: Loyalty vs. Honesty
A close colleague, who is also a good friend outside of work, is taking office supplies for personal use. You notice this but are hesitant to report it because of your personal relationship. Office theft has been a rising concern, and the company is cracking down.

Roles:
Employee who notices the theft
Colleague stealing supplies
HR representative

Case Study 5: Workplace Equality vs. Client Preferences
A major client prefers working with male employees and has subtly hinted they'd take their business elsewhere if they have to deal with female account managers. Your boss is considering assigning only male staff to this client.

Roles:
Boss
Female Account Manager
Male Account Manager

Case Study 6: Product Quality vs. Timelines
Your team is on a tight deadline to ship out a software product. During the final review, you notice a bug. Fixing it would mean missing the deadline. Shipping it on time might mean unsatisfied customers.

Roles:
Team Lead
Software Developer who found the bug
Marketing executive

Chapter 9: Leadership in Different Contexts

Leadership is not a monolithic concept confined to a specific setting, but rather a multifaceted tapestry woven through various sectors and spheres of influence. Whether we examine the tenacity of personal leadership, the dynamics within collaborative teams, the broad vision required for organizational leadership, or the nuanced dance of politics and social movements, leadership takes on different hues and intensities. This chapter dives deep into these contexts, revealing both the shared principles and distinct intricacies of leadership across them.

The realm of personal leadership explores the inward journey of an individual, the self-awareness, self-regulation, and the alignment of one's values with actions. It's about understanding oneself as a leader and recognizing the innate potential that resides within, waiting to be channeled effectively.

As we move to team leadership, the canvas broadens. It's no longer just about individual prowess but about fostering a cohesive environment where diverse members come together, blending their strengths and talents. Here, leaders not only navigate the waters of collaboration and conflict but also orchestrate the symphony of collective achievement.

Organizational leadership expands the horizon even further, demanding a strategic lens and the ability to manage change, culture, and growth on a grand scale. It's about painting a vision for an entire organization and ensuring that every cog in the machine moves synchronously towards that envisioned future.

In politics, leaders grapple with a unique set of challenges: the balance of personal conviction with public service, the interplay of power and ethics, and the perpetual limelight that scrutinizes every decision. It's a domain where leadership is not just about direction but also about representation.

Leadership within nonprofits and social movements underscores the mission-driven spirit. Here, leaders rally causes, mobilize resources, and champion societal changes, often against significant odds. Their leadership is a testament to the power of passion, perseverance, and purpose.

As we journey through this chapter, a comparative analysis will weave threads between these diverse contexts, illuminating the universal tenets of leadership while also celebrating its unique manifestations. In the evolving landscape of the 21st century, where boundaries blur and contexts continuously shift, understanding leadership in its varied forms becomes paramount.

Personal Leadership

At the heart of all forms of leadership lies the individual. Before one can effectively guide a team, steer an organization, or influence a nation, there is a fundamental necessity to lead oneself. Personal leadership is, therefore, foundational, setting the tone for every other form of leadership one might aspire to. It's a journey inward, focusing on introspection, reflection, and personal growth.

Understanding oneself as a leader is the initial step. Each person possesses a unique combination of strengths, vulnerabilities, experiences, and aspirations. Recognizing these intrinsic traits and understanding how they shape one's leadership style is vital. Some may be charismatic orators, while others excel in quiet diplomacy. Some may be risk-takers, ever eager to innovate, while others offer the stability of careful deliberation. The key is not to emulate another's style but to harness one's genuine attributes in leadership.

The journey of self-awareness and self-regulation delves deeper into this self-understanding. Self-awareness involves recognizing one's emotions, triggers, and biases. It's about understanding one's reactions and the implications they have on others. Self-regulation, on the other hand, focuses on managing these reactions. A leader who can navigate their emotional landscape can make decisions that are balanced and measured, rather than being reactionary. This emotional intelligence not only enhances personal leadership but also fosters trust and respect among those they lead.

Setting personal goals and aligning them with values is the compass of personal leadership. It's easy to drift in the vast sea of opportunities and challenges, but a clear set of goals anchored to one's core values provides direction. These goals are not just about achievements but also about personal growth and contribution. They reflect the leader's vision for themselves, the mark they wish to leave, and the legacy they aspire to build. Moreover, when personal goals resonate with deeply held values, the path of leadership becomes not just a pursuit but a passion.

Personal leadership is the bedrock upon which all other leadership forms are built. It is a continual process of introspection, growth, and realignment. As we venture into broader contexts of leadership in subsequent sections, the principles of personal leadership remain ever relevant, reminding us that the most profound leadership journeys often begin within.

Team Leadership

Transitioning from personal leadership to guiding a collective group heralds a new set of challenges and opportunities. Leading a team isn't just about magnifying one's individual capabilities but harnessing the collective strength, talent, and diversity of the team members. It's about fostering an environment where every member feels valued, understood, and empowered. This transition is encapsulated in the realm of team leadership.

Characteristics of effective team leaders are manifold. While personal leadership traits remain foundational, leading a team requires additional attributes. An effective team leader is often a great communicator, ensuring that every member is aligned with the team's goals and objectives. They're also adept at recognizing the unique strengths and weaknesses of each team member and delegating tasks accordingly. Moreover, empathy plays a crucial role. Understanding team members' aspirations, challenges, and concerns and addressing them proactively can make the difference between a disengaged group and a cohesive team.

Building cohesive, collaborative, and high-performing teams requires intentional effort. Cohesion is fostered when team members feel a sense of belonging and trust. This trust isn't just in the leader, but also among the team members themselves. Leaders can promote this by creating opportunities for team members to collaborate, share their insights, and learn from one another. Celebrating collective successes, acknowledging individual contributions, and ensuring transparent communication are key components of this effort. It's also about setting clear expectations and providing the tools and resources necessary for the team to succeed.

Navigating team dynamics, conflicts, and decision-making processes is perhaps the most intricate aspect of team leadership. No two individuals are alike, and when diverse personalities and viewpoints come together, conflicts are inevitable. However, conflicts, when managed constructively, can lead to innovative solutions and deeper team bonds. Effective team leaders not only anticipate these dynamics but also mediate disagreements in a way that ensures every voice is heard. In terms of decision-making, they strike a balance between assertiveness and consensus-building. They recognize when to take charge and when to step back and let the team arrive at a collective decision.

Team leadership is a multifaceted role that demands a blend of interpersonal skills, strategic thinking, and adaptability. While the challenges are many, the rewards of leading a motivated, high-performing team towards shared objectives are unparalleled. As the landscape of leadership broadens further, the principles of team leadership offer insights and lessons that apply to even larger contexts.

Organizational Leadership

As we ascend the ladder of leadership dimensions, we arrive at a broader, more encompassing domain: organizational leadership. This level of leadership transcends the boundaries of individual or team dynamics and delves into the intricate web of entire organizations. Organizational leaders often find themselves at the helm of vast ships, tasked with steering these entities towards uncharted waters while ensuring the wellbeing of all aboard.

The role and responsibilities of organizational leaders are vast and varied. Beyond the day-to-day management of their organization's functions, they are the torchbearers of the organization's vision, mission, and values. Their decisions have ripple effects, influencing not just immediate teams but departments, stakeholders, and often the wider community or industry. Their responsibility is not just to lead but to inspire, to not just manage but to innovate. Their decisions need to consider the immediate needs of the organization while also being forward-thinking, anticipating future challenges and opportunities.

Strategic visioning and organizational alignment are pivotal facets of organizational leadership. It's not enough to have a vision; leaders must ensure that this vision is clear, compelling, and communicated effectively throughout the organization. Every team, department, and individual should understand their role in realizing this vision. This requires aligning organizational structures, processes, and culture with the strategic goals. It's a continuous process of checking the pulse of the organization, recalibrating strategies, and ensuring that resources are optimally utilized towards achieving these goals.

Managing organizational change and evolution is another crucial aspect. In today's fast-paced world, change is the only constant.

Organizational leaders must be adept at recognizing the winds of change early on and preparing their organization to adapt. This could mean technological upgrades, shifts in business models, mergers, or even pivoting to entirely new directions. Leading an organization through such changes is no small feat. It requires a combination of strategic foresight, effective communication, and the ability to rally the entire organization towards new objectives. Moreover, leaders must be cognizant of the human side of change, understanding and addressing the anxieties, apprehensions, and aspirations of their employees as they navigate these transitions.

Political Leadership

Stepping onto the global stage, political leadership introduces a realm where the stakes are profoundly high, and the repercussions of decisions often echo through generations. Unlike many other forms of leadership where the primary focus might be a specific organization or cause, political leaders hold the weight of entire nations, populations, and at times, global coalitions on their shoulders. This realm is rife with complexities, shaped by a confluence of history, culture, geopolitics, and the ever-evolving tapestry of human aspirations.

At the heart of the unique challenges of leading in the political arena is the intricate dance of diplomacy and governance. Here, leaders are not just managing teams or organizations; they are helming nations, navigating intricacies of policy, diplomacy, national interests, and international relations. Their decisions can impact economies, peace treaties, and even the course of history. The challenges range from internal pressures of party politics to the larger issues of global geopolitics, international diplomacy, and even the unforeseen events that test a nation's mettle and resilience.

Balancing personal convictions with public demands and expectations is another core aspect of political leadership. While every leader enters the arena with personal convictions and beliefs, the nature of democratic systems requires a constant ear to the ground. Leaders must strike a balance between what they believe is right for the nation's future and the immediate needs and demands of their constituents. This balancing act is delicate and fraught with challenges, as decisions might not always align with popular sentiment. It's about making tough choices, often choosing between the lesser of two evils, all while staying true to one's core values and the larger vision for the nation.

To genuinely grasp the intricacies of political leadership, it's illuminating to explore the journeys of both men and women who have left indelible marks on the pages of history. Delving into the case studies of such leaders reveals the breadth and depth of their experiences, challenges, strategies, and the consequent legacies they've bestowed upon the world.

Leaders like Nelson Mandela stand as towering figures, representing resilience, vision, and an unwavering spirit of reconciliation in the face of immense adversities. His leadership journey, from the prison cells of Robben Island to the presidential office of South Africa, is a testament to the power of purpose, patience, and perseverance.

Winston Churchill is another paradigm of leadership, particularly during the tumultuous times of World War II. His speeches stirred nations, his decisions steered the course of battles, and his resilience provided hope in the darkest hours. Churchill's leadership was marked not just by strategic brilliance but also by an oratory power that galvanized a nation.

Indira Gandhi, the first female prime minister of India, offers a compelling study in leadership, particularly in the context of a nation grappling with post-colonial challenges. Her tenure was a blend of bold decisions, from the liberation of Bangladesh to the controversial Emergency. Gandhi's leadership was characterized by a mix of determination, vision, and at times, contentious choices that continue to be debated today.

In the pantheon of influential female political leaders, figures like Golda Meir and Margaret Thatcher also hold prominent positions. Meir, often referred to as the "Iron Lady of Israel," showcased a leadership style marked by tenacity and a deep commitment to the state of Israel. On the other hand, Margaret Thatcher, Britain's first female prime minister, was known for her uncompromising politics and policies, earning her both admiration and criticism.

Contemporary female leaders like Jacinda Ardern, New Zealand's prime minister, are setting new paradigms. Ardern's compassionate and decisive leadership, particularly in the face of crises like the Christchurch Mosque shootings or the COVID-19 pandemic, provides fresh insights into the evolving nature of political leadership in the 21st century.

Studying these leaders' trajectories provides invaluable insights into the multifaceted nature of political leadership. Their stories encompass a spectrum of challenges, decisions, victories, and setbacks. For budding political leaders, these narratives are not just historical accounts but powerful lessons, serving as both cautionary tales and profound sources of inspiration.

Leadership in Nonprofits and Social Movements

Navigating the leadership terrain in nonprofits and social movements presents a unique set of challenges and rewards. While many leadership principles apply universally across sectors, the nonprofit realm, with its mission-driven focus, demands a nuanced approach. Effective leaders in this space must blend passion with pragmatism, vision with viability, and inspiration with implementation.

The mission-driven nature of nonprofit leadership distinguishes it from its for-profit counterparts. At its core, leadership in this sector is about effecting change, be it social, environmental, cultural, or political. The mission serves as the North Star, guiding every strategic decision and action. This unwavering commitment to a cause often requires leaders to adopt a selfless demeanor, placing the organization's goals and the community's needs above personal aspirations or profit motives.

Mobilizing resources, volunteers, and community engagement becomes a pivotal task for nonprofit leaders. Unlike the corporate world, where financial metrics often dictate decisions, nonprofits must rely on a mix of donor contributions, grants, and community support. Leaders in this space become adept at storytelling, translating the nonprofit's mission into compelling narratives that resonate with potential donors, volunteers, and beneficiaries. Moreover, given the often-limited resources, nonprofit leaders are required to be innovative, maximizing impact with minimal means. Engaging volunteers, often the lifeblood of many nonprofits, necessitates a different skill set. It's about igniting passion, fostering a sense of belonging, and recognizing contributions that go beyond monetary compensations.

Effective leadership in pivotal social movements provide a lens through which we can understand the profound impact of leadership in mobilizing masses and effecting change. Leaders like Martin Luther King Jr., who spearheaded the American Civil Rights Movement, showcased the power of nonviolent resistance, eloquence, and moral fortitude. His "I Have a Dream" speech remains an enduring testament to visionary leadership. Similarly, Malala Yousafzai's brave stand against the Taliban's repression in Pakistan and her advocacy for girls' education has made her an icon of resilience and advocacy worldwide.

In a different context, Greta Thunberg, a teenage environmental activist, galvanized global attention towards climate change. Her ability to inspire millions and mobilize them for climate strikes demonstrates the changing face of leadership in social movements, especially in the digital age.

These leaders, among many others, underline the essence of leadership in nonprofits and social movements. Their journeys offer insights into the complexities, challenges, and, most importantly, the transformative power of leadership dedicated to a cause larger than oneself.

Comparative Analysis: Leadership Across Contexts

Leadership, though universally acknowledged and revered, takes on different hues and tones depending on the context in which it unfolds. From the personal sphere, where leadership might be more introspective and centered on self-growth, to the vast political arena where decisions influence nations, the tenets and challenges of leadership exhibit both stark contrasts and surprising similarities. Understanding these nuances becomes instrumental for leaders as they navigate different terrains or seek to adapt lessons from one realm to another.

Highlighting Key Differences and Similarities in Leadership Roles

At a glance, personal leadership seems worlds apart from, say, leadership in a vast corporate conglomerate or a political setting. Personal leadership is often about self-awareness, setting personal milestones, and being a leader in one's life narrative. In contrast, organizational or political leadership involves steering complex entities, managing multifaceted teams, and making decisions that impact large numbers of people.

However, look a bit closer, and the overlaps begin to emerge. The self-awareness crucial in personal leadership is equally vital for a CEO or a political leader, ensuring they remain grounded, empathetic, and visionary. The goal setting that one does in personal leadership mirrors the strategic planning and vision-setting in organizational contexts.

Drawing Lessons from One Context to Another

Understanding these parallels allows for a cross-pollination of ideas and strategies. For instance, the reflective practices nurtured in personal leadership can be integrated into team-building exercises in organizational settings, fostering team cohesion and alignment. On the other hand, the structured decision-making processes employed in corporations can be adapted for personal goal setting, making objectives clearer and more attainable. Navigating team dynamics and conflicts in organizational leadership can provide valuable lessons for personal leadership, especially when working collaboratively on projects or community initiatives.

Identifying Universal Leadership Principles and Practices

Despite the variances across contexts, some leadership principles remain timeless and universal. Integrity, for instance, is a cornerstone, whether one is leading oneself, a team, or a nation. Similarly, effective communication, empathy, resilience in the face of challenges, and the ability to inspire and motivate are attributes that resonate across all leadership domains.

While the contexts may dictate specific roles, responsibilities, and challenges, the heart of leadership – guiding, influencing, and inspiring – remains constant. Recognizing this universality, while also appreciating the unique nuances of each context, can empower leaders to be more adaptable, insightful, and effective, irrespective of the arena they find themselves in.
Future Trends in Contextual Leadership

As we stand on the cusp of a rapidly changing world, driven by technological innovations, socio-political shifts, and evolving global dynamics, the canvas of leadership too is undergoing a transformation. The way leadership is perceived, enacted, and evaluated in different contexts is bound to shift, bringing with it a slew of challenges and opportunities. To remain effective and relevant, leaders must be attuned to these changes and be agile in adapting their approaches and strategies.

The Evolving Nature of Leadership Roles in Different Domains:

☐ Digital and Remote Leadership: With remote work and digital transformations becoming the norm rather than the exception, leaders must be adept at managing geographically dispersed teams, utilizing digital tools for communication and collaboration, and fostering a sense of unity and culture in virtual environments.

☐ Eco-Leadership: As the planet grapples with climate change and environmental challenges, leaders across sectors will increasingly need to embody eco-leadership, emphasizing sustainability, eco-friendly practices, and a commitment to the planet's welfare.

☐ Human-Centric Leadership: With artificial intelligence and automation on the rise, there's a growing emphasis on the human element in leadership. Leaders will be called upon to prioritize emotional intelligence, empathy, and well-being, ensuring that the human spirit thrives amid technological advancements.

Anticipating Challenges and Opportunities in the Coming Decade

☐ Cultural Agility: As the world becomes more interconnected, leaders will encounter diverse cultures, beliefs, and perspectives. This demands cultural agility – the ability to understand, respect, and work effectively across cultures.

☐ Ethical Quandaries: Rapid technological advancements, especially in areas like biotechnology, AI, and data analytics, will present leaders with complex ethical dilemmas. Navigating these with integrity will be paramount.

☐ Opportunity in Crisis: The coming decade, like any other, will have its share of global crises – be it economic downturns, health pandemics, or geopolitical tensions. Leaders who can see opportunity in adversity, innovating and guiding their teams through tumultuous times, will be particularly valued.

Preparing for Leadership in Emerging Contexts

☐ Lifelong Learning: The future will belong to leaders who are perpetual learners, constantly updating their knowledge and skills, staying abreast of global trends, and being open to unlearning and relearning.

☐ Building Diverse Networks: Engaging with a diverse set of people, from different industries, cultures, and backgrounds, can offer leaders fresh perspectives, insights, and collaborative opportunities.

☐ Mental Agility: The ability to think critically, adapt to changing situations, and envision multiple scenarios will be crucial. This mental agility will allow leaders to pivot their strategies as per the demands of the situation.

As we navigate through the expansive realm of leadership in varied contexts, from personal spaces to the global political arena, some truths emerge resplendent. Leadership, in its myriad forms, may manifest differently across settings, but certain core principles bind these distinct roles together. Our journey through this chapter has been one of discovery, uncovering the facets that make a leader truly effective regardless of their domain.

Synthesizing insights from these diverse leadership roles teaches us that while techniques and strategies might differ, the essence of leadership remains consistent: vision, empathy, integrity, and the ability to inspire. A political leader might rally masses with their charisma just as a personal leader might motivate themselves with inner resilience; the core remains the same. It's about driving positive change, building relationships, and leaving an indelible mark.

Adaptable, resilient, and context-aware leadership stands out as more than just desirable traits; they are imperative in today's volatile, uncertain, complex, and ambiguous world. Leaders who are rigid in their approaches or lack adaptability risk becoming obsolete, failing to resonate with their teams or constituents. Resilience, on the other hand, ensures that leaders remain unflinchable in the face of challenges, bouncing back with even greater determination. Being context-aware allows leaders to truly understand the unique dynamics of their environment, be it a nonprofit organization, a political rally, or a corporate boardroom, and tailor their leadership style accordingly.

One of the most enduring lessons we glean from studying leadership across contexts is the paramount importance of continuous learning and growth. Leadership isn't a static achievement; it's an evolving journey. The landscapes of challenges and opportunities are in constant flux, and leaders must evolve in tandem. This requires an unquenchable thirst for knowledge, a commitment to self-improvement, and the humility to recognize that no matter how accomplished, there's always room for growth.

Exercises and Activities for Chapter 9: Leadership in Different Contexts

Role-playing in Different Leadership Roles

Objective: To understand the nuances of leadership roles in various contexts by immersing oneself in simulated scenarios.

Personal Leadership Scenario: Participants draft a personal leadership vision statement and share it with a partner, receiving feedback.

Team Leadership Scenario: Divide participants into small groups and assign each group a team challenge. One person takes on the leadership role and navigates the team through the challenge.

Political Leadership Scenario: Participants are provided with a hypothetical political situation. They must address their 'constituents' (other participants) on how they would handle the situation.

Analyzing Real-life Case Studies across Contexts

Objective: To derive insights and lessons from the journeys and decisions of leaders in diverse scenarios.

Case Study on Organizational Leadership: Analyze the leadership approach of Satya Nadella at Microsoft and his role in its transformation.

Case Study on Political Leadership: Examine the leadership traits and strategies of Angela Merkel during her tenure as the Chancellor of Germany.

Case Study on Nonprofit Leadership: Investigate the impact and leadership style of Malala Yousafzai and her efforts in promoting education for girls.

Group Discussions on Contextual Leadership Challenges and Opportunities

Objective: To facilitate an exchange of ideas and perspectives on the distinct challenges and opportunities in various leadership contexts.

Discussion on Personal Leadership: Reflect on personal experiences where participants felt they took on a leadership role, even if unofficially. What were the challenges? What did they learn?

Discussion on Team Leadership: Share experiences of being part of a team. What leadership qualities did they appreciate in their team leaders? What qualities were lacking?

Discussion on Political Leadership: Debate the pros and cons of various political leadership styles observed globally. What are the inherent challenges in political leadership compared to other forms?

Feedback and Reflection

Objective: After the exercises, participants reflect on their experiences, discuss key takeaways, and provide feedback. Ask participants to jot down three key lessons they've derived from the role-playing, case studies, and discussions.

Chapter 10: The Future of Leadership

In a world that is in constant flux, leadership remains the lighthouse guiding organizations, nations, and communities towards progress, resilience, and innovation. However, as the landscape of our society and technology changes, so does the nature of leadership. This chapter embarks on a journey into the future of leadership—a realm marked by rapid technological advancements, global challenges of unprecedented scales, and an ever-increasing need for sustainable approaches.

Beginning with "Leadership in a Digital Age," we explore the profound implications of the fourth industrial revolution on leadership. How does one lead in a world where artificial intelligence, virtual reality, and digital networks redefine communication, decision-making, and even the very nature of work? What skills and mindsets will the leaders of tomorrow need to navigate this brave new world?

As we progress into "Global Challenges and Leadership," the focus shifts to the intricate tapestry of global dynamics. Leaders of the future won't merely be guiding local or organizational entities but will have to understand and address global crises, ranging from climate change to geopolitical tensions, and from resource scarcity to large-scale migrations. The interconnected nature of our world demands leaders who can think globally while acting locally.

"Sustainable Leadership" delves into a leadership approach for the long run. In an era where immediate results often overshadow long-term strategies, how can leaders foster sustainability? How can they ensure that their decisions not only cater to the present but also pave the way for a brighter, more sustainable future for the next generations?

Prepare to embark on an enlightening expedition into what the future holds for leadership, understanding its challenges and arming oneself with the knowledge and perspective needed to lead in the coming decades.

The digital revolution is much more than just new tools or technologies—it's a transformative force reshaping how we think, work, communicate, and lead. Leaders in this age need to grapple with the multifaceted dimensions of digital transformation and its profound implications.

Digital Transformation and Its Implications for Leaders

Digital transformation has rippled through every industry, redefining the way we conceive, execute, and evaluate business models. For leaders, understanding this transformation is not just a matter of keeping up with the latest tech trends; it's about grasping the profound shifts in business paradigms and customer expectations brought about by this digital revolution.

Digital transformation reshapes customer expectations. As digital experiences become more seamless and personalized in consumer lives, they naturally expect the same level of convenience and customization from businesses. Leaders must thus be acutely tuned to these evolving expectations, ensuring that their organizations can offer exceptional, digitally enabled customer experiences.

The very nature of competition changes in a digitally transformed environment. Traditional competitors might be supplanted by new, digital-first entrants or even companies from entirely different sectors that leverage digital platforms to enter new markets. Leaders must maintain a panoramic view of the competitive landscape, identifying potential threats from non-traditional sources and seizing cross-industry collaboration opportunities.

This transformation also brings about a renewed focus on data. With the proliferation of digital touchpoints, organizations now have access to a treasure trove of data. Leaders need to foster a data-driven culture where insights are actively harvested and applied for strategic advantage. However, with great data comes great responsibility. Ethical considerations around data usage, storage, and privacy become paramount. Leaders must ensure robust cybersecurity measures are in place and champion transparent, responsible data practices.

Organizational structures and work cultures are not immune to the effects of digital transformation either. Hierarchies may flatten, and agile, cross-functional teams might become the norm. The concept of a fixed workplace might blur as remote working technologies allow teams to collaborate from across the globe. Leaders must be adept at managing these distributed teams, ensuring that despite physical distances, the organizational culture remains cohesive and aligned with its core values.

As rapid technological advancements become the norm, there's an underlying challenge of ensuring that the human element isn't lost amidst the algorithms and automations. Leaders must strike a balance, ensuring that while technology streamlines and optimizes processes, the human touch, empathy, and intuition remain integral to decision-making and customer interactions.

The implications of digital transformation for leaders are vast and multifaceted. It requires them to be visionaries, strategists, culture-builders, and ethical guardians, all while navigating the uncharted waters of the digital age. The leaders who can meld the digital with the human, who can innovate while staying rooted in core values, are the ones who will truly steer their organizations into a promising, digitally augmented future.

Leading Remote and Hybrid Teams

Leading remote and hybrid teams is a modern leadership challenge that presents both exciting opportunities and intricate hurdles. The promise of casting a wider net in talent acquisition, drawing from a global pool, is contrasted with the challenge of knitting together a cohesive, unified team from individuals who might never share physical space.

At the foundation of leading remote teams lies trust. In traditional office settings, trust could be built through daily interactions, casual coffee breaks, or spontaneous team lunches. However, in a remote setting, these organic touchpoints are absent. Leaders must, therefore, be deliberate in cultivating trust. This begins with giving team members the autonomy to manage their tasks and time, resisting the urge to micromanage, and emphasizing outcomes over the number of hours logged in. Regular check-ins, where the focus is not just on task updates but also on individual well-being, can also bolster trust and camaraderie.

Collaboration is another crucial pillar. Thanks to technological advancements, there's an array of digital tools designed to foster collaboration in remote teams—from video conferencing software to project management tools. But more than the tools themselves, leaders need to instill a culture where collaboration is encouraged and celebrated. This might involve setting clear communication norms, encouraging knowledge sharing, and perhaps even organizing periodic virtual brainstorming sessions where team members can pool their diverse perspectives.

One potential pitfall of remote work is the feeling of isolation that team members might experience. Without the regular hum of office chatter or the possibility of a colleague dropping by for a quick chat, remote work can sometimes feel solitary. Leaders must be attuned to this. Organizing virtual team-building activities, encouraging informal virtual coffee chats, or even periodic in-person meet-ups (if feasible) can mitigate these feelings of isolation.

Furthermore, the hybrid model—where some team members work from the office while others are remote—brings its own set of challenges. The risk here is creating a two-tier system where remote workers feel like secondary members. Leaders must be vigilant to ensure parity in communication, access to resources, and opportunities for growth, irrespective of where a team member is located.

Diversity is another facet to consider. Remote and hybrid teams often draw members from diverse cultural, geographical, and linguistic backgrounds. While this diversity can be a tremendous asset, bringing in varied perspectives and approaches, it also demands leaders be culturally sensitive. Understanding different cultural nuances, being aware of potential language barriers, and even being considerate of time zones during scheduling are all markers of effective leadership in such contexts.

Navigating the Challenges of the Information Era

The advent of the information era has radically transformed the leadership landscape. No longer are leaders solely reliant on hierarchical structures or limited data; instead, they're now submerged in a deluge of real-time information from myriad sources. This presents both unparalleled opportunities and daunting challenges.

One of the most striking features of the information era is its democratizing effect. Information, which was once the purview of a select few, is now accessible to many. This shifts the balance of power and requires leaders to be more collaborative and inclusive in their decision-making. The mantra has evolved from "knowledge is power" to "sharing knowledge is power."

This immense accessibility to information also comes with its pitfalls. The sheer volume can be overwhelming. Every day, leaders are bombarded with reports, analytics, news, and updates.

The challenge is to distill this vast amount of information into actionable insights. This requires a combination of critical thinking, discernment, and an analytical mindset. It's about distinguishing the signal from the noise and making informed decisions that align with the organization's overarching objectives.

Adding to the complexity is the prevalence of misinformation and disinformation. In the digital realm, where information can be disseminated widely with just a click, leaders must be vigilant about the sources they rely upon. They must cultivate a healthy skepticism, fact-checking and cross-referencing information before making pivotal decisions. It's equally essential to foster a culture where team members feel empowered to question and validate information, ensuring that the organization isn't swayed by half-truths or outright falsehoods.

The rapidity with which information flows also means that the business environment is in a constant state of flux. Leaders can no longer afford to be static or overly rigid in their strategies. Agility and adaptability become paramount. This doesn't mean being whimsical or constantly changing course but rather being attuned to shifts in the environment and being prepared to pivot when necessary. It's about having a clear vision but being flexible in the routes taken to achieve that vision.

The information era has also magnified the significance of transparency in leadership. With stakeholders having access to vast amounts of data and information, leaders are under increased scrutiny. Authenticity, openness, and accountability become cornerstones of effective leadership in this era. Leaders must be proactive in communicating, addressing concerns, and showcasing both successes and lessons learned from failures.

The information era, with its vast reservoirs of data and rapid dissemination channels, has redefined leadership. It demands a new breed of leaders – ones who are discerning, agile, transparent, and collaborative. While the challenges are manifold, so are the opportunities. Leaders who can adeptly navigate this intricate landscape will be at the forefront of driving progress, innovation, and sustainable growth in their organizations.

Digital Ethics, Privacy, and Cybersecurity in Leadership

Navigating the digital realm is no longer just about leveraging technology for operational efficiency or market advantage; it's equally about ensuring ethical practices in this new landscape. Digital ethics touches on the very essence of how organizations conduct themselves online, and leaders are at the forefront of establishing and upholding these standards.

The digital realm has amplified the reach and impact of decisions. A single data breach can not only affect a company's bottom line but can irreparably tarnish its reputation. Likewise, the misuse of customer data can lead to loss of trust, which is paramount in the digital age. For leaders, this means that ethical considerations are not just supplementary; they are central to business strategy.

Privacy has emerged as a cornerstone of digital ethics. With organizations collecting vast amounts of data, how this data is handled, stored, and used becomes critical. Leaders need to prioritize the protection of user data, ensuring it's used only for its intended purpose. Moreover, transparency in data practices is crucial. Users should know what data is being collected, why it's being collected, and how it's being used. Organizations should be proactive in communicating their data policies and obtaining informed consent.

Cybersecurity is another vital facet of digital leadership. As cyber threats become more sophisticated, leaders need to be abreast of the latest security measures and ensure that their organizations are fortified against potential breaches. This isn't just about having the right technology in place; it's about cultivating a culture of cybersecurity awareness. Every team member, from entry-level to senior leadership, should be educated about the importance of cybersecurity and the role they play in safeguarding the organization's digital assets.

Leaders also need to address the ethical implications of emerging technologies. From artificial intelligence to biometrics, new technologies often tread a fine line between innovation and ethical concerns. Leaders must be discerning, critically assessing the implications of these technologies and ensuring that their deployment aligns with the organization's ethical stance and the broader societal expectations.

The digital realm is a space where boundaries blur—between personal and professional, between public and private. Leaders, more than ever, need to exemplify ethical behavior, knowing that their actions online can and will be scrutinized. Their digital footprint serves as a testament to their character and the values they espouse.

Global Challenges and Leadership

In an era marked by unprecedented interconnectedness, the very definition of leadership has evolved. Today's leaders aren't just navigating their immediate environments; they're steering through a vast and intricate global landscape, fraught with challenges but also ripe with opportunities.

The advancements in communication technologies and transportation have knit the world closer than ever before. Businesses can now cater to audiences worldwide, collaborations span continents, and events in one corner of the globe can ripple out, affecting economies and societies thousands of miles away. However, with this interconnectedness comes a set of challenges. Information overload, the rapid spread of misinformation, the juxtaposition of diverse cultures, and global competition are just a few of the hurdle's leaders must clear.

As businesses expand their horizons, leaders find themselves at the helm of diverse teams, each member bringing their unique cultural nuances. It is crucial for leaders to cultivate cultural intelligence, recognizing, respecting, and leveraging the diverse perspectives that multicultural teams offer. It's not just about avoiding misunderstandings but about embracing diversity as a potent source of innovation.

The past few decades have underscored the unpredictable nature of global challenges. Whether it's the far-reaching consequences of financial downturns or the global implications of health crises like the COVID-19 pandemic, leaders must be equipped to steer their organizations through tumultuous times. This demands foresight, adaptability, resilience, and a commitment to making decisions grounded in both data and empathy.

Leading in a global context is both an art and a science. It requires leaders to expand their purview, considering the global implications of their decisions, while also staying deeply rooted in their local contexts, understanding the immediate needs and nuances of their communities. It's a delicate balance, but one that's essential in our increasingly globalized world.

Sustainable Leadership

The conversation around sustainability has long transcended the realm of environmental concerns. While the conversation indeed originated in the domain of environmentalism, it now encompasses the very fabric of leadership across sectors and industries. Sustainable leadership goes beyond the conventional definition of sustainability—it is about laying foundations today for a resilient, thriving future.

At its core, sustainable leadership means prioritizing longevity over quick wins. In a world driven by quarterly earnings and short-term metrics, this can be a challenging paradigm shift. Yet, sustainable leaders understand the importance of balancing immediate results with a long-term vision. It's not about dismissing the significance of achieving immediate goals; instead, it's about ensuring that these short-term achievements do not come at the expense of long-term success and stability.

One cannot discuss sustainable leadership without touching upon ethics and corporate social responsibility. These elements have become cornerstones for modern businesses. Stakeholders, from customers to investors, increasingly evaluate companies based on their ethical stances and contributions to societal betterment. Here, leaders play a pivotal role. They're the ones setting the tone, making pivotal decisions, and ensuring alignment between organizational values and actions.

Sustainable leadership also brings to the fore the critical discussion around environmental sustainability. As the global community grapples with the consequences of climate change, leaders are in a unique position to drive positive change. By championing green initiatives, reducing waste, and promoting sustainable practices, leaders can not only reduce their organizations' environmental footprints but also inspire others to follow suit.

Sustainable leadership extends to the realm of social equity. As societal conversations around inequality and justice gain momentum, leaders must be at the forefront, championing inclusivity, diversity, and fairness. This is not just about 'doing the right thing'; diverse and inclusive teams are shown to be more innovative, resilient, and high performing.

Sustainable leadership is about foresight, responsibility, and holistic thinking. Leaders who embrace this philosophy do not merely react to the present but proactively shape the future, ensuring that their leadership leaves a lasting, positive legacy for generations to come.

Through the lens of history, theory, practice, and future anticipation, it becomes evident that leadership is neither stagnant nor predictable. Instead, it is a constantly evolving tapestry, interwoven with the threads of societal shifts, technological advances, and the timeless principles of human connection.

Reflecting on the journey undertaken through these pages, several key takeaways emerge. Firstly, the future of leadership is not just about understanding or predicting what tomorrow might hold. It's about having the adaptability and resilience to navigate the unknown, making informed decisions even in the face of uncertainty. It requires leaders to possess both the foresight to anticipate challenges and the agility to pivot as circumstances dictate.

For all the change and uncertainty that the future might bring, the essence of leadership remains rooted in a few timeless truths. At its core, leadership is about influencing and guiding others towards a shared goal. It's about building trust, fostering collaboration, and creating an environment where every individual feels valued and empowered. These principles, though simple, are profound in their impact and will remain relevant regardless of the epoch or era.

Another salient reflection is the indispensable value of continuous learning. The leaders of tomorrow will not just be those with a wealth of knowledge but those with an insatiable curiosity. In a world that's rapidly changing, the most valuable currency is not necessarily what you know, but how you learn. Embracing a mindset of perpetual growth, where every experience becomes an opportunity for learning and reflection, will be paramount.

As we turn our gaze to the horizon, we recognize the immense responsibility resting on the shoulders of the next generation of leaders. To them, we offer not just the knowledge contained in this text but a clarion call to action. The challenges of the future will demand leaders who are not only prepared and proactive but deeply principled. Leaders who, beyond strategy and vision, are anchored by a strong moral compass, guiding their decisions and actions.

Leadership, in all its grandeur, is not just about leading others. It's a journey of self-discovery, of understanding one's values, strengths, and purpose. It's about leaving a legacy, making an indelible mark on the sands of time. To all aspiring leaders reading this: may you lead with heart, with purpose, and with the unwavering belief that you can create a positive difference in this world. The future beckons, and it is bright with promise.

References

Introduction

Bass, B. M. (1999). Two decades of research and development in transformational leadership. European Journal of Work and Organizational Psychology, 8(1), 9-32.

Cialdini, R. B. (2001). Influence: Science and practice (4th ed.). Boston: Allyn & Bacon.

Fiedler, F. E. (1967). A theory of leadership effectiveness. New York: McGraw-Hill.

Festinger, L. (1957). A theory of cognitive dissonance. Stanford, CA: Stanford University Press.

Goleman, D. (1995). Emotional intelligence. New York: Bantam.

Greenleaf, R. K. (1977). Servant leadership: A journey into the nature of legitimate power and greatness. Mahwah, NJ: Paulist Press.

Janis, I. L. (1972). Victims of groupthink. Boston: Houghton Mifflin.

Kahneman, D., & Tversky, A. (1984). Choices, values, and frames. American Psychologist, 39(4), 341.

Lewin, K., Lippitt, R., & White, R. K. (1939). Patterns of aggressive behavior in experimentally created social climates. Journal of Social Psychology, 10, 271-299.

Maslow, A. H. (1943). A theory of human motivation. Psychological Review, 50, 370-396.

Northouse, P. G. (2018). Leadership: Theory and practice (8th ed.). Thousand Oaks, CA: Sage Publications.

Shannon, C. E., & Weaver, W. (1949). The mathematical theory of communication. Urbana: University of Illinois Press.

Stogdill, R. M. (1948). Personal factors associated with leadership: A survey of the literature. Journal of Psychology, 25, 35-71.

Tversky, A., & Kahneman, D. (1974). Judgment under uncertainty: Heuristics and biases. Science, 185, 1124-1131.

Yukl, G. (2012). Leadership in organizations (8th ed.). Upper Saddle River, NJ: Prentice Hall.

Zaccaro, S. J. (2007). Trait-based perspectives of leadership. American Psychologist, 62(1), 6.

Zigarmi, P., & Roberts, T. P. (2017). Leadership strategies for creating a high-involvement workplace. Journal of Leadership Studies, 10(4), 6-15.

Chapter 1

Chemers, M. M. (1997). An integrative theory of leadership. Lawrence Erlbaum Associates Publishers.

Covey, S. R. (1990). The Seven Habits of Highly Effective People: Restoring the Character Ethic. New York: Free Press.

Drucker, P. (2001). The Essential Drucker: Selections from the Management Works of Peter F. Drucker. New York: HarperBusiness.

Gardner, H. (1995). Leading Minds: An Anatomy of Leadership. Basic Books.

Goleman, D. (2000). Leadership that gets results. Harvard Business Review, 78(2), 78-90.

Heifetz, R. A. (1994). Leadership without easy answers. Cambridge, MA: Belknap Press.

Kouzes, J. M., & Posner, B. Z. (1995). The Leadership Challenge: How to Make Extraordinary Things Happen in Organizations. San Francisco: Jossey-Bass.

Maxwell, J. C. (1993). Developing the Leader Within You. Nashville, TN: Thomas Nelson.

Northouse, P. G. (2015). Leadership: Theory and Practice. Los Angeles: Sage Publications.

Rost, J. C. (1991). Leadership for the Twenty-First Century. New York: Praeger.

Senge, P. M. (1990). The Fifth Discipline: The Art & Practice of The Learning Organization. Doubleday.

Shamir, B., House, R. J., & Arthur, M. B. (1993). The motivational effects of charismatic leadership: A self-concept-based theory. Organization Science, 4(4), 577-594.

Yukl, G. (2012). Leadership in Organizations. Upper Saddle River, NJ: Prentice Hall.

Zaleznik, A. (1977). Managers and leaders: Are they different? Harvard Business Review, 55(5), 67-78

Chapter 2

Avolio, B. J., & Gardner, W. L. (2005). Authentic leadership development: Getting to the root of positive forms of leadership. The Leadership Quarterly, 16(3), 315-338.

Bass, B. M. (1985). Leadership and performance beyond expectations. Free Press.

Blake, R. R., & Mouton, J. S. (1964). The managerial grid. Houston, TX: Gulf Publishing Co.

Brown, M. E., & Treviño, L. K. (2006). Ethical leadership: A review and future directions. The Leadership Quarterly, 17(6), 595-616.

Burns, J. M. (1978). Leadership. New York: Harper & Row.

Carlyle, T. (1841). On Heroes, Hero-Worship, and The Heroic in History. London: James Fraser.

Fiedler, F. E. (1967). A theory of leadership effectiveness. New York: McGraw-Hill.

Greenleaf, R. K. (1977). Servant leadership: A journey into the nature of legitimate power and greatness. Paulist Press.

Gronn, P. (2002). Distributed leadership as a unit of analysis. The Leadership Quarterly, 13(4), 423-451.

Hersey, P., & Blanchard, K. H. (1969). Life cycle theory of leadership. Training & Development Journal.

House, R. J., Hanges, P. J., Javidan, M., Dorfman, P. W., & Gupta, V. (2004). Culture, Leadership, and Organizations: The GLOBE Study of 62 Societies. Thousand Oaks: Sage Publications.

Stogdill, R. M. (1948). Personal factors associated with leadership: A survey of the literature. Journal of Psychology, 25, 35-71.

Chapter 3

Bar-On, R. (1997). Emotional quotient inventory: Technical manual. Toronto, Canada: Multi-Health Systems.

Bass, B. M., & Riggio, R. E. (2006). Transformational leadership. Psychology Press.

Costa, P. T., & McCrae, R. R. (1992). Revised NEO Personality Inventory (NEO-PI-R) and NEO Five-Factor Inventory (NEO-FFI) manual. Odessa, FL: Psychological Assessment Resources.

Furnham, A., Richards, S. C., & Paulhus, D. L. (2013). The Dark Triad of personality: A 10-year review. Social and Personality Psychology Compass, 7(3), 199-216.

Goleman, D. (1995). Emotional intelligence. New York: Bantam Books.

Greenleaf, R. K. (1977). Servant leadership: A journey into the nature of legitimate power and greatness. Paulist Press.

Judge, T. A., Bono, J. E., Ilies, R., & Gerhardt, M. W. (2002). Personality and leadership: A qualitative and quantitative review. Journal of Applied Psychology, 87(4), 765-780.

Mayer, J. D., & Salovey, P. (1997). What is emotional intelligence? In P. Salovey & D. Sluyter (Eds.), Emotional development and emotional intelligence: Educational implications (pp. 3-34). Basic Books.

Paulhus, D. L., & Williams, K. M. (2002). The Dark Triad of personality: Narcissism, Machiavellianism, and psychopathy. Journal of Research in Personality, 36(6), 556-563.

Rosenthal, S. A., & Pittinsky, T. L. (2006). Narcissistic leadership. The Leadership Quarterly, 17(6), 617-633.

Salovey, P., & Mayer, J. D. (1990). Emotional intelligence. Imagination, Cognition, and Personality, 9(3), 185-211.

Smith, M. B., Bruner, J. S., & White, R. W. (1956). Opinions and personality. New York: Wiley.

Van Vugt, M., Hogan, R., & Kaiser, R. B. (2008). Leadership, followership, and evolution: Some lessons from the past. American Psychologist, 63(3), 182-196.

Chapter 4

Asch, S. E. (1951). Effects of group pressure upon the modification and distortion of judgments. Carnegie Press.

Bass, B. M., & Bass, R. (2008). The Bass Handbook of Leadership: Theory, Research, and Managerial Applications. Free Press.

Cialdini, R. B. (2001). Influence: Science and practice (4th ed.). Boston: Allyn & Bacon.

Festinger, L. (1957). A theory of cognitive dissonance. Stanford University Press.

French, J. R., & Raven, B. (1959). The bases of social power. In D. Cartwright (Ed.), Studies in Social Power (pp. 150-167). Institute for Social Research.

Janis, I. L. (1972). Victims of groupthink. Boston: Houghton Mifflin.

Keltner, D., Gruenfeld, D. H., & Anderson, C. (2003). Power, approach, and inhibition. Psychological Review, 110(2), 265-284.

Lewin, K. (1947). Frontiers in group dynamics: Concept, method and reality in social science; social equilibria and social change. Human Relations, 1(1), 5-41.

Milgram, S. (1974). Obedience to authority: An experimental view. Harpercollins.

Sherif, M. (1936). The psychology of social norms. Harper & Brothers.

Tajfel, H., & Turner, J. C. (1979). An integrative theory of intergroup conflict. In W. G. Austin & S. Worchel (Eds.), The social psychology of intergroup relations (pp. 33-47). Brooks/Cole.

Tannenbaum, A. S. (1968). Control in organizations. McGraw-Hill.

Tuckman, B. W. (1965). Developmental sequence in small groups. Psychological Bulletin, 63(6), 384-399.

Weber, M. (1947). The theory of social and economic organization. Free Press.

Yukl, G. (2012). Leadership in organizations (8th ed.). Prentice Hall.

Zimbardo, P. G. (2007). The Lucifer effect: Understanding how good people turn evil. Random House.

Chapter 5

Adler, N. J. (1997). International dimensions of organizational behavior (3rd ed.). South-Western Cengage Learning.

Catalyst. (2007). The double-bind dilemma for women in leadership: Damned if you do, doomed if you don't. Catalyst Inc.

Cox, T. (1994). Cultural diversity in organizations: Theory, research, and practice. Berrett-Koehler Publishers.

Eagly, A. H., & Carli, L. L. (2007). Through the labyrinth: The truth about how women become leaders. Harvard Business School Press.

Gudykunst, W. B. (2005). Theorizing about intercultural communication. SAGE Publications.

Hofstede, G., & Hofstede, G. J. (2005). Cultures and organizations: Software of the mind (2nd ed.). McGraw-Hill.
House, R. J., Hanges, P. J., Javidan, M., Dorfman, P. W., & Gupta,

V. (2004). Culture, leadership, and organizations: The GLOBE study of 62 societies. SAGE Publications.

Ibarra, H., Ely, R., & Kolb, D. (2013). Women rising: The unseen barriers. Harvard Business Review, 91(9), 60-66.

Kanter, R. M. (1977). Men and women of the corporation. Basic Books.

Kimmel, M. (2017). The gendered society. Oxford University Press.

Morrison, A. M., White, R. P., & Van Velsor, E. (1992). Breaking the glass ceiling: Can women reach the top of America's largest corporations? Addison-Wesley.

Nkomo, S. M. (1992). The emperor has no clothes: Rewriting "race in organizations." The Academy of Management Review, 17(3), 487-513.

Northouse, P. G. (2018). Leadership: Theory and practice (8th ed.). SAGE Publications.

Rosener, J. B. (1990). Ways women lead. Harvard Business Review, 68(6), 119-125.

Sandberg, S. (2013). Lean in: Women, work, and the will to lead. Knopf.

Triandis, H. C. (2006). Cultural intelligence in organizations. Group & Organization Management, 31(1), 20-26.

Chapter 6

Argyris, C., & Schön, D. A. (1978). Organizational learning: A theory of action perspective. Addison-Wesley.

Daft, R. L. (2017). Organization theory & design (12th ed.). Cengage Learning.

Festinger, L. (1957). A theory of cognitive dissonance. Stanford University Press.

Greenberg, J., & Baron, R. A. (2008). Behavior in organizations (9th ed.). Pearson/Prentice Hall.

Hackman, J. R., & Wageman, R. (2005). A theory of team coaching. Academy of Management Review, 30(2), 269-287.

Herzberg, F. (1966). Work and the nature of man. World Publishing.

Judge, T. A., & Robbins, S. P. (2017). Essentials of organizational behavior (14th ed.). Pearson.

Kanter, R. M. (1983). The change masters: Innovation & entrepreneurship in the American corporation. Simon & Schuster.

Lewin, K. (1947). Frontiers in group dynamics. Human Relations, 1(1), 5-41.

Maslow, A. H. (1943). A theory of human motivation. Psychological Review, 50(4), 370-396.

Robbins, S. P., & Coulter, M. (2016). Management (13th ed.). Pearson.

Schein, E. H. (2010). Organizational culture and leadership (4th ed.). Jossey-Bass.

Chapter 7

Bandura, A. (1977). Social learning theory. Prentice-Hall.

Collins, J. C. (2001). Good to great: Why some companies make the leap... and others don't. Harper Business.

Covey, S. R. (1989). The 7 habits of highly effective people. Free Press.

Drucker, P. F. (2007). The essential Drucker. Harpercollins.

Gladwell, M. (2000). The tipping point: How little things can make a big difference. Little, Brown and Company.

Heifetz, R. A., & Linsky, M. (2002). Leadership on the line: Staying alive through the dangers of leading. Harvard Business Review Press.

Herzberg, F. (1987). One more time: How do you motivate employees?. Harvard Business Review, 65(5), 109-120.

Kotter, J. P. (1996). Leading change. Harvard Business Press.

Locke, E. A., & Latham, G. P. (2002). Building a practically useful theory of goal setting and task motivation. American Psychologist, 57(9), 705.

Mintzberg, H. (1979). The structuring of organizations. Prentice-Hall.

Pink, D. H. (2009). Drive: The surprising truth about what motivates us. Riverhead Books.

Porter, M. E. (1985). Competitive advantage: Creating and sustaining superior performance. Free Press.

Senge, P. M. (1990). The fifth discipline: The art & practice of the learning organization. Doubleday.

Tuckman, B. W. (1965). Developmental sequence in small groups. Psychological Bulletin, 63(6), 384.
Yukl, G. A. (2012). Leadership in organizations (8th ed.). Pearson.

Chapter 8

Badaracco, J. L. (2002). Leading quietly: An unorthodox guide to doing the right thing. Harvard Business Press.

Bass, B. M., & Steidlmeier, P. (1999). Ethics, character, and authentic transformational leadership behavior. Leadership Quarterly, 10(2), 181-217.

Brown, M. E., Treviño, L. K., & Harrison, D. A. (2005). Ethical leadership: A social learning perspective for construct development and testing. Organizational Behavior and Human Decision Processes, 97(2), 117-134.

Ciulla, J. B. (Ed.). (2004). Ethics, the heart of leadership (2nd ed.). Praeger.

Greenleaf, R. K. (1977). Servant leadership: A journey into the nature of legitimate power and greatness. Paulist Press.

Kidder, R. M. (2005). Moral courage: Taking action when your values are put to the test. HarperCollins.

Kohlberg, L. (1981). Essays on moral development, Vol. I: The philosophy of moral development. Harper & Row.

Northouse, P. G. (2018). Ethical leadership. In Leadership: Theory and practice (8th ed., pp. 359-390). Sage Publications.

Price, T. L. (2008). Leadership ethics: An introduction. Cambridge University Press.

Rest, J. R. (1986). Moral development: Advances in research and theory. Praeger.

Treviño, L. K., & Brown, M. E. (2004). Managing to be ethical: Debunking five business ethics myths. Academy of Management Executive, 18(2), 69-81.

Werhane, P. H. (2008). Moral imagination and the search for ethical decision-making in management. Ruffin Series in Business Ethics, 219-234.

Yukl, G., Mahsud, R., Hassan, S., & Prussia, G. E. (2013). An improved measure of ethical leadership. Journal of Leadership & Organizational Studies, 20(1), 38-48.

Chapter 9

Avolio, B. J., & Yammarino, F. J. (Eds.). (2013). Transformational and charismatic leadership: The road ahead. Emerald Group Publishing.

Bass, B. M., & Riggio, R. E. (2006). Transformational leadership (2nd ed.). Psychology Press.

Burns, J. M. (1978). Leadership. Harper & Row.

Chait, R. P., Ryan, W. P., & Taylor, B. E. (2011). Governance as leadership: Reframing the work of nonprofit boards. John Wiley & Sons.

Chemers, M. M. (2014). An integrative theory of leadership. Psychology Press.

Conger, J. A. (1999). Charismatic and transformational leadership in organizations: An insider's perspective on these developing streams of research. Leadership Quarterly, 10(2), 145-179.

Crosby, B. C., & Bryson, J. M. (2018). Leadership for the common good: Tackling public problems in a shared-power world (3rd ed.). Jossey-Bass.

Heifetz, R. A. (1994). Leadership without easy answers. Harvard University Press.

Hollander, E. P. (2012). Inclusive leadership: The essential leader-follower relationship. Routledge.

Kanter, R. M. (2011). SuperCorp: How Vanguard Companies Create Innovation, Profits, Growth, and Social Good. Crown Business.

Kotter, J. P. (2012). Leading change. Harvard Business Press.

Mintzberg, H. (2009). Managing. Berrett-Koehler Publishers.

Morse, R. S., Buss, T. F., & Kinghorn, C. M. (2007). Transformative public leadership: A new paradigm for the 21st century. Public Administration Review, 67(5), 779-787.

O'Toole, J., Galbraith, J., & Lawler III, E. E. (2002). When two (or more) heads are better than one: The promise and pitfalls of shared leadership. California Management Review, 44(4), 65-83.

Tichy, N. M., & Cohen, E. (2002). The leadership engine: How winning companies build leaders at every level. HarperCollins.

Warren, D. I. (1976). The American community college: A reconsideration. Jossey-Bass.

Yukl, G. (2010). Leadership in organizations (7th ed.). Prentice Hall.

Chapter 10

Avolio, B. J., Walumbwa, F. O., & Weber, T. J. (2009). Leadership: Current theories, research, and future directions. Annual Review of Psychology, 60, 421-449.

Bennis, W. (2009). On becoming a leader. Basic Books.

Bower, J. L., & Yves, D. L. (2011). The future of leadership. Harvard Business Review.

Cogliser, C. C., & Brigham, K. H. (2004). The intersection of leadership and entrepreneurship: Mutual lessons to be learned. The Leadership Quarterly, 15(6), 771-799.

Drucker, P. F. (2008). Management challenges for the 21st century. HarperCollins.

Ferdig, M. A. (2007). Sustainability leadership: Co-creating a sustainable future. Journal of Change Management, 7(1), 25-35.

Hanna, N. K. (2017). Transformation of global development: Emerging trends and future implications. Rowman & Littlefield.

Heifetz, R., Grashow, A., & Linsky, M. (2009). The practice of adaptive leadership: Tools and tactics for changing your organization and the world. Harvard Business Press.

Kanter, R. M. (2012). Evolve!: Succeeding in the digital culture of tomorrow. Harvard Business Press.

Mendenhall, M. E., Osland, J., Bird, A., Oddou, G. R., & Maznevski, M. L. (2012). Global leadership: Research, practice, and development (2nd ed.). Routledge.

Pfeffer, J. (2010). Power play. Harvard Business Review, 88(7/8), 84-92.

Ready, D. A., Hill, L. A., & Conger, J. A. (2008). Winning the race for talent in emerging markets. Harvard Business Review, 86(11), 62.

Senge, P. M., Smith, B., Kruschwitz, N., Laur, J., & Schley, S. (2008). The necessary revolution: How individuals and organizations are working together to create a sustainable world. Doubleday.

Tapscott, D., & Williams, A. D. (2008). Wikinomics: How mass collaboration changes everything. Portfolio.

Wheatley, M. (2007). Leadership in the age of complexity: From hero to host. Resurgence Magazine.